Tae Kwon Do

TECHNIQUES & TRAINING

Kyong Myong Lee

Sterling Publishing Co., Inc.   New York

Translated by Elisabeth Reinersmann

Photo Credits
All photos by Dieter Birkner,
except pages 2 and 40: K. M. Lee (Archives)

Library of Congress Cataloging-in-Publication Data

Lee, Kyong Myong.
    [Richtig Taekwondo. English]
    Tae kwon do : techniques & training / Kyong Myong Lee.
        p.   cm.
    Includes index.
    ISBN 0-8069-5955-X
    1. Tae kwon do.   2. Tae kwon do—Training.   I. Title.
GV1114.9.L44   1996
796.8′153—dc20   95-52503
                                                          CIP

10   9   8   7   6   5   4   3   2   1

Published 1996 by Sterling Publishing Company, Inc.
387 Park Avenue South, New York, N.Y. 10016
Originally published and © 1995 by
BLV Verlagsgesellschaft mbH, Munich
under the title *Richtig Taekwondo*
English translation © 1996 by Sterling Publishing Co., Inc.
Distributed in Canada by Sterling Publishing
 Canadian Manda Group, One Atlantic Avenue, Suite 105
Toronto, Ontario, Canada M6K 3E7
Distributed in Great Britain and Europe by Cassell PLC
Wellington House, 125 Strand, London WC2R OBB, England
Distributed in Australia by Capricorn Link (Australia) Pty Ltd.
P.O. Box 6651, Baulkham Hills, Business Centre, NSW 2153, Australia
Manufactured in the United States of America
All rights reserved

Sterling ISBN 0-8069-5955-X

Kyong Myong Lee was born in Pusan, Korea, in 1939 and began studying the sport of tae kwon do when he was 14 years old. After receiving his B.A. in philosophy from Yonsei University in Seoul he worked as a journalist and writer, having several books published. However, he also developed an increasing interest in tae kwon do, being especially drawn to the spiritual–philosophical aspect of the sport, as well as the demands on physical conditioning.

In 1967 Kyong Myong Lee moved to Austria, where much of his time was devoted to the promotion of tae kwon do. He was a true pioneer of his native sport, not only in Austria but also in Germany and Poland. He returned to Seoul, Korea, in 1991, where he is now Secretary General of the World Tae Kwon Do Federation (WTF).

He continues to write and is still doing research in self-defense exercises, with special emphasis on tae kwon do.

Contents

Introduction — 4

What Is Tae Kwon Do? — 4
What Does Tae Kwon Do "Do"? — 4
The Inner Meaning of Tae Kwon Do — 6
Tae Kwon Do & Athletics — 7

The Development of Tae Kwon Do — 8

Historical Background — 8

General Techniques & Training — 11

The Dynamics of Tae Kwon Do — 11
Tae Kwon Do Training — 14
What Is "Do"? — 16
Dojang (Training Space) — 17
Kyong-Ye (Paying Respect) — 18
Kihop (Concentrated Power) — 18

Basic Skills — 19

Overview of Tae Kwon Do Techniques — 19
Sogi (Stance) — 19
Maggi (Blocking, Defense) — 23
Konggyokki (Attacking Techniques) — 26
Overview of Attacking Techniques — 30
Poom & Poomse — 31

Technique Combinations — 32

Combinations of Basic Techniques — 32
Han-bon Gyoroogi (Practicing Compulsory Sparring with a Partner) — 32
Baal-jit-ki (Stepping Techniques) — 35

Countertechniques — 37
Hosinsool (The Art of Self-Defense) — 38
Kyukpa (Breaking Test) — 40

Competition — 41

Positions Assumed in Competition — 41
Suggestions for Competitors — 42
Tips to Prevent Injuries — 42
Situations Demanding Tactical Response — 43

Performance of Poomse Forms — 45

Pal-Gwe — 46
Tae-Kook — 46
Koryo — 46
Kum-Kang — 47
Tae-Book — 47
Meanings of the Exercise Diagrams (Planview Sequence of Movements) — 48
Training Recommendations — 49

Practice Section — 50

Pal-Gwe 1–8 Chang — 50
Tae-Kook 1–8 Chang — 88
Koryo — 122
Kum-Kang — 128
Tae-Book — 134

Glossary of Korean Terms — 141

Index — 143

Introduction

What Is Tae Kwon Do?

Freely translated, *tae kwon do* means "the art of kicking and punching (with hands and feet)." Literally, it means:

tae	pushing, jumping, or crushing with the foot;
kwon	hitting or crushing with fist or hand;
do	the Way, the story, the art.

In summary, tae kwon do is a technique of unarmed self-defense, using both hands and feet to evade or deflect an opponent swiftly or to stage a quick counterattack.

Tae kwon do differs from the many other kinds of karate mainly in the hand techniques. Other karate techniques prefer the use of the feet, but the characteristics distinguishing tae kwon do are numerous. Nothing really compares to what tae kwon do has to offer.

What Does Tae Kwon Do "Do"?

The Korean art of self-defense, tae kwon do, has been developed independently over the last 20 centuries. One characteristic of tae kwon do is that an attack is countered without a weapon, which means only hands or feet are used as defense. All movements in tae kwon do are based strictly on the concept of self-defense. There is barely a part of the human body that could not be used as defensive weapon: hands, fingers, fists, ankle, elbow, knee, feet, head, and so on.

Training regularly improves overall well-being, brings about a healthy emotional and physical balance, increases agility and flexibility, and improves the skill of viewing things with better detachment.

Tae kwon do improves not only physical strength but also discipline and focused thinking. Without such skills it is impossible to gain self-confidence and the composure necessary for a successful defense.

> Self-confidence is a prerequisite for humility and tolerance, two of the goals of tae kwon do.

A healthy body is active and resilient. Psychological and physical self-confidence affects all relationships, be they between individuals, within the family, or among neighbors and countries.

Tae kwon do as a whole consists of a system of forms and combinations of movements termed *poomse*, along with fighting (*gyoroogi*) and breaking (*kyukpa*) techniques. It requires great concentration, which, in turn, may result in almost unbelievable power. Tae kwon do poomse forms consist of different positions of the feet combined with defensive hand techniques, as well as punches carried out with feet or fists. These elements flow into and complement each other, comprising the form as a whole and representing the defense against one or several opponents.

The most well-known poomse forms are:

- *pal gwe* 1 to 8 *chang,*
- *tae kook* 1 to 8 *chang,*
- *koryo,*
- *kum-kang,*
- *tae-book.*

The forms for the advanced degree-(*dan-*) holding practitioner:

- *pyongwon,*
- *shipjin,*
- *jitae,*
- *chonkwon,*
- *hansoo,*
- *ilyo.*

We distinguish between two types of competition: One is a freestyle sparring form, *jayu gyoroogi,* where the techniques of defense and counterattack can be used in any sequence or combination of the participant's choosing. The second type of competition is conducted according to a predetermined format.

The predetermined, or compulsory, program (*han-bon gyoroogi*) is particularly useful for training purposes because mistakes and careless moves can be corrected immediately.

Every student must be able to perform these forms perfectly before he can participate in freestyle gyoroogi competition.

In actual competition—and without a thorough knowledge of all aspects of the sport—it is impossible to use full force against an opponent without causing injury or even death. Being able to successfully split a wooden board, shatter a brick or rock—practiced during training—is proof that a student is successfully focusing his or her power and energy on one specific spot, demonstrating convincingly what is possible if mind and body are coordinated in a meaningful way.

The clothes worn when doing tae kwon do—called the *dobok* (dough-bahk) in Korean and a *gi* (ghee) in Japanese—are designed to accommodate all necessary movements. The dobok is white, signifying moral purity and beginning according to Zen philosophy. Belts (called *Ty* in Korean) worn around the dobok come in different colors and identify the different levels of accomplishment of students:

white	= Beginner	
yellow	= 10 and 9 Gup (Class)	
green	= 8 and 7 Gup	Student Level
blue	= 6 and 5 Gup	
brown	= 4 and 3 Gup	
red	= 2 and 1 Gup	
red/black	= 1–3 Poom	Master Level (under 15 years old)
black	= 1–10 Dan (Degree)	1–5 Master Level
		6–10 Grand Master Level

Introduction

The Inner Meaning of Tae Kwon Do

Tae Kwon Do—More Than Movement

Tae kwon do is the physical expression of the human will for survival as well as a tool for helping a person fulfill his or her spiritual goals. All movements in tae kwon do are based on the adoption of an attitude for protection against attacks and the will to defend oneself. As these physical needs were expressed, they were linked with the addition of a positive mental acuity. And together they may lead—at the last stage of perfection—to a triumph over the ego, giving the sport a philosophical dimension.

The Emotional Significance

A person in good health generally has a great amount of energy. Someone in poor health, on the other hand, may have little drive for work. Much more than a matter of intellect, our inclination is very much connected to how we feel, which also affects how we behave.

When doing tae kwon do all organs are activated, muscles are developed and the brain is stimulated, which in turn, in the widest sense of the word, strengthens a person's willpower. Simply surviving hasn't made everybody happy—we all are looking for meaning in our lives that will give us energy and drive. Tae kwon do cultivates willpower and self-confidence through a combination of physical and mental conditioning.

Tae Kwon Do—a Means of Character Development

Our body is subject to physical laws and, in a sense, can be viewed as a machine that grows, develops, and moves. This "machine" is doing its work by changing into different positions as different situations arise. From a mental point of view, the "machine" is thinking—it has an idea and looks for a solution through a process akin to mental training.

We distinguish between light workouts and high-performance workouts. The latter supports a strong will to fight and the former is simply a means to positively influence the circulatory system.

Tae kwon do builds character, a strong will, and vigor that will result in the ability to meet all of life's situations with well-balanced and directed energy. Disciplined energy and a strong will to live (fighting spirit) instill confidence under any circumstances, allowing a person to approach things calmly and with confidence, with inner peace. If in the process the ego can be overcome—in the sense that one is prepared to sacrifice one's own inclination and behavior while, at the same time, being able to be humble—the following will have been accomplished:

- the basis for an ethical and exemplary way of life;
- fulfillment of one of the key characteristics necessary for becoming a leader in the community.

Tae Kwon Do & Athletics

Tae Kwon Do—a Physically Complete Sport

People participate in sports activities for many different reasons. These range from wanting to join a particular group and its activities to the desire through fitness and movement to prolong one's life. The motive includes achieving physical fitness as well as the need for psychological balance.

Tae kwon do can be viewed as an answer to the demands of everyday life while at the same time providing us with a guide for our behavior towards ourselves and others. The sport is a system of movements and positions that in a systematic and controlled way involves the whole body. It is for these reasons that this sport has become an important means for integrating mind, body, and spirit through a total fitness program.

Tae Kwon Do Turns Extremities into Weapons

Tae kwon do is such a powerful sport that it is very dangerous for a practitioner to test its effectiveness on another person. The idea is to use one's expertise only to defend against an unexpected attack. There is respect for the principle of self-defense, because, for the trained practitioner, fists turn into hammers, fingers to sharp arrow points, and the outside of the hand into the edge of a knife, and feet can assume the power of a sledgehammer.

There are fundamental ways for fists, hands, and feet to become such weapons, and there are also some very specific ways that these "body weapons" are used. Some movements are contained in several forms: quick-reaction movements, where body and extremities are moving to the right, the left, backwards, or forwards, and are used for defense as well as for counterattacks. Some movements are practiced alone, and others are done with a partner, where the hitting and kicking defense against such attacks are practiced.

When all fundamental compulsory movements can be performed smoothly the tae kwon do student is ready to learn the freestyle forms of the sport. Freestyle is so dangerous that students must wear specific equipment for the protection of certain parts of the body. This type of tae kwon do must never be practiced with people who are not familiar with the sport. Experts only demonstrate their skills by smashing bricks, roof tiles, wooden boards, or similar objects. Objects may be thrown in midair and the athlete smashes them while jumping.

The Development of Tae Kwon Do

Historical Background

The people of ancient Korea—just as others around the world—constantly sought to improve their capacity to secure food and to defend themselves against attack. Over time, they invented tools that made both gathering food and self-defense easier. But even after they had mastered new weapons, they never ceased training mind and body, inventing games and holding competitions.

Tae Kwon Do During the Koguryo Dynasty

As early as the Neolithic Age, different tribes in various parts of ancient Korea were holding organized games as part of their religious practices. Over time these exercises underwent many adaptations, serving not only as a means to stay healthy but also to augment and improve fighting skills.

The experience of dealing with wild animals along with careful observation of how these animals defended themselves and carried out an attack led people to mimic their movements, creating in the process, in the region of ancient Korea, a very effective system of fighting. The result was the evolution of a form called *taekyon*—an ancient term for tae kwon do.

The beginning of tae kwon do can be traced to the kingdom of Koguryo, founded in the region that is now North Korea in the first century B.C. Paintings on the ceilings of tombs from that period include tae kwon do motifs. These paintings were discovered in 1935 by Japanese archeologists in the royal tombs of Muyong-chong and Kakchu-chong in Tungku (Hwando province in Manchuria), which was the capital city of Koguryo. Whereas the painting in the Muyong-chong tomb depicts two men facing each other engaged in freestyle tae kwon do, the painting in Kakchu-chong shows what appear to be two wrestlers.

The Japanese historian Tatashi Saito writes in his *Studies of the Culture of Ancient Korea* that these paintings tell us that either the deceased person buried in the tomb had practiced an ancient form of tae kwon do during his lifetime or that—accompanied by singing and dancing—others engaged in this activity in an effort to console the soul of the deceased in his afterlife.

Hwarang Do During the Silla Dynasty

The kingdom of Silla, located in the southeastern part of the Korean peninsula, was founded in the third century A.D. Two Buddhist stone reliefs guarding the famous tomb built by Kim Dae Sung (A.D. 751–774) in the cave of Suckkool-am near Kyongyu, the capital of Silla, serve as documentation. These carved figures greet visitors in the *Kumkang maggi* posture, a defensive movement that is still used today in tae kwon do.

The people in Silla were almost entirely dedicated to hunting and to studying the art of fighting—called *hwarang do*—in order to perfect mind and body. As Silla struggled with Koguryo to the north and the kingdom of Paekche to the west, the system of hwarang do played a vital role, along with assistance from the T'ang Dynasty of China, in the unification of ancient Korea under the Silla Dynasty in A.D. 668.

The Connection to Chinese Kung Fu and Japanese Karate

Many believe that tae kwon do has its roots in the Chinese self-defense method of kung fu. The Buddhist saint Dharma, one of the most famous religious leaders from India, came to China in A.D. 520 and spent nine years at the Hsiaolin Temple (in the province of Honan) where, among other things, he taught and promoted kung fu, a kind of exercise regimen. The ceiling paintings in the royal tombs of Koguryo in ancient Korea, however, have been dated from between A.D. 3 and 427. This supports the conclusion that tae kwon do did not strictly grow out of the kung fu tradition.

The actual beginnings of karate—a self-defense sport from Japan—has never been established; however, two stories of its origin are often argued.

One is that one of the members of the Chinese Chen Yuanpin immigrated to Japan late during the Chinese Ming Dynasty (A.D. 1368–1644) and he promoted kung fu there. The other version claims there is proof that karate is an extension and further development of a form called *okinawate*, a type of self-defense practiced in the Okinawan islands (now part of Japan). How old okinawate is has not been determined. Clues to its origin may be found on a close reading of the historical records from the royal house of Choson during the Korean Yi Dynasty (1392–1910), in which it is mentioned that delegates from the Ryukyu (Okinawan) islands came regularly to pay tribute to the king of Choson.

During the Yi Dynasty the martial art *soo bak do*—an early name for tae kwon do—was very popular; some hypothesize that the delegates from the Okinawan islands were introduced to and learned soo bak do, taking it back to their homeland on their return. This speculation does have a parallel in the Korean *Nu* (another type of game) that was transported to become a popular sport on the Okinawan islands.

Soo Bak Do During the Koryo Dynasty

Earlier, during the Koryo Dynasty (A.D. 918–1392) soo bak do was not only viewed as a healthy form of exercise but also it is was respected greatly for its value in training the military.

9

The Development of Tae Kwon Do

The following examples from historical documents show how popular and respected this early form of tae kwon do was:

"King Uijong admired the excellence of Yi Ui-min in soo bak and promoted him from *taejong* [military rank] to *pyolchang*."

"The King visited the Sang-chun pavilion and attended the soo bak competition."

"The King followed the soo bak competition in the Hwa-Bi palace."

"The King came to Ma-am to watch the soo bak competition."

From these reports it seems that soo bak do competition was also a great attraction for spectators.

It is thought that soo bak do reached its highest popularity during the Koryo Dynasty under the reign of King Uijong (A.D. 1147–1170). This is about the same time that kung fu was very popular in China (the Sung Dynasty, A.D. 960–1279). Two different systems developed, *neikya* and *weikya,* that placed different emphases on defensive and offensive skills. Such evidence seems to show that tae kwon do may not have originated solely in Korea, and that, in the long history of the region, it has subsequently undergone its own independent development.

Another historical document reports that people from the neighboring provinces of Cholla and Chungchong met at Chakji, a small border town, in order to determine the best soo bak do fighter. This report supports the belief that soo bak do was already a popular sport in the distant past. Those who wanted to become a royal guard underwent rigorous tests, soo bak do being one of the major examinations.

The importance of soo bak do during the first half of the Yi Dynasty is underscored by the publication of an illustrated book about martial arts, in which soo bak do occupies the most important chapter. The author was King Chongjo himself—which indicates that soo bak do was not only a favorite sport of the population at large but was also very important at the royal house. During the second half of the Yi Dynasty soo bak do lost some of its popularity. Historians have suggested that this was due to a power struggle between the royal houses, which left less time for athletic events and recreation and put more emphasis on the politics of the day. However, it is thought that soo bak do continued to be a favorite recreational activity among the populace.

The Dynamics of Tae Kwon Do

The more athletes there are who practice and excel at tae kwon do, the more important it is that they have a thorough understanding of the principles of physics that underlie the sport. There are two reasons for this: an experienced athlete with such knowledge is better able to assess the effectiveness of certain actions and thereby increase his or her awareness of what he or she is trying to learn; and this, in turn, makes learning new techniques much easier. Principles of physics illuminate two of the key elements in the performance of tae kwon do: one is the process of the *transfer of energy,* the other is the requirement for *balance.* Success or failure of a defensive or offensive move can be easily understood by analyzing both these elements, energy and balance.

Three Newtonian Principles & Their Importance for Tae Kwon Do

The first of the three deals with the difference between matter at rest and matter in motion—also called the *law of inertia.* Every body remains in a state of rest or in uniform straight-line motion unless acted upon by an external force. This qualitative principle states that energy is necessary in order to set a body in motion that is at rest.

The second principle is the *law of mechanics.* It gives information about the size of the force and shows the character of the vector of the force. It says: a change in the direction of an object's movement caused by a force that is acting on it is proportional and takes place along the line the force is moving in. This is also—and much better—described by the formula

$$F = m \times a$$

(F = force, m = mass, a = acceleration).

The characteristic of the speed or impulse—p—is the product of the mass—m—and the speed—v. A change in direction changes the quality of the impulse. The change in speed is caused by a force, and the greater the force F is, the greater the change of the impulse.

When the second Newtonian principle is applied to tae kwon do, mass m means the body of the attacker or the defender; and the acceleration a is the change in speed of the mass during the moment of contact between the two bodies.

The third principle states that any force initiated by body "A" and affecting body "B" will influence the former when it hits by producing a force that is equal but in the opposite direction. This concept is better known under the abbreviated form of: action = reaction. Both bodies "A" and "B", in this context, are the bodies of the attacker and the defender. If the attacker directs a force, either with his fist or foot, against the body of an opponent, an equally strong force is generated by the defender that is moving in an identical line but in the direction of the attacker.

Balance & Stability

The stability of a body depends, for the most part, on three factors:

- weight (or mass),
- the size of the surface supporting that body,
- the distance between the center of gravity of the body and the supporting surface.

The center of gravity of a body is a point which can be physically or mathematically determined by imagining the total body mass. If a body becomes unstable, the force F, acting at the center of gravity, is greater than the product of body weight—G—and the horizontal distance a between the body's center of gravity at the tilting edge, divided by the height—h—the distance between the center of the body and the supporting surface. Refer to the drawing below.

It seems clear that to improve the stability of a body, the supporting surface must either be increased or the center of gravity of the body must be lowered. During competition both happen when the participant lunges one leg forward. This, however, is a defensive posture that does diminish mobility. A sudden attack can be carried out more easily if the degree of stability is less. How, then, is one to get into an offensive or defensive position that is effective yet based on principles of physics?

A sudden attack is most effective when not only fists and feet move with lightning speed but, simultaneously, the total body mass is moving in the direction of the target. This is the *law of mechanics* in action: the attack is carried out with great force.

The opponent defends himself by increasing his stability in order not to lose his balance through the force of the attack. It is important that the supporting surface effectively absorb the increased force.

Speed

Mass by itself, even if it increases the degree of effectiveness, can never generate useful force if it is not accompanied by speed. When tae kwon do practitioners talk about a *solid step* and a *light step*, these terms always

Schematic illustration of balance.

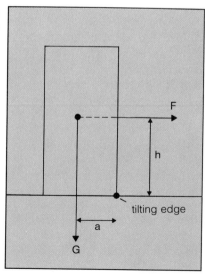

F

h

tilting edge

a

G

refer to the *speed* with which a movement is carried out. A solid step is always carried out with high speed, whereas a light step is always slow. There are several ways by which a practitioner can increase the speed of a body movement. One way is by effectively shifting the center of gravity of the body, which, however, always reduces the relative stability of the stance. Another way is by increasing the distance to the target, thereby increasing the amount of speed that is generated. Increasing the distance to the target also requires added agility on the part of the athlete.

The Nervous System

While bones and joints are the basic structure of the human body, it is the nervous system that guides the actions of the muscles. It is the movements of the individual parts of the body and the speed of the reaction time that determine the degree of swiftness of the action—in offensive as well as a defensive situations.

The nervous system branches throughout the body into increasingly smaller and smaller strands. Each stimulus to any part of the nervous system is passed on to the central nervous system. In addition, certain groups of nerves are designed to initiate certain muscle movements. The force created by the body will only reach its greatest potential if all groups of nerves involved work in a coordinated fashion. A contributing factor in coordinating specific nerve segments is mental concentration. The connecting path between individual nerves is important for the signal's reaching its destination. At the beginning of training an athlete is not yet able to control and coordinate these connections, and caution, therefore, should be taken. However, over time and with consistent training these usually unconscious reactions can be and are influenced.

Breathing & "Ki"

The general technique for any sport is to exhale when bending down or turning and to inhale when the body straightens up. In tae kwon do the practitioner is also taught to exhale when executing a hit or kick and to hold his or her breath at the instant the hit or kick makes contact, in order to achieve maximum effectiveness. The reason for this particular breathing technique is that exhalation reduces the internal resistance and allows the body to be more flexible; furthermore, it seems that the most power behind a hit or kick is achieved when the breath is held.

Shouting "*Kihop*" when an arm or foot makes contact serves to push the air out of the lungs, which at the same time assists the practitioner in concentrating on that moment. However, if the shout is too soon or long—before the target has been reached—the practitioner will not be able to generate

13

sufficient force because the most important aspect is mental concentration at the moment of impact.

Without this concentration and control of the breathing process, attack as well as defense reactions cannot be carried out successfully. In learning the sport it is therefore necessary (1) to engage in long and intensive training with the aid of your mind in order to achieve the desired coordination of internal processes, as well as (2) to learn the proper breathing technique—ultimately allowing your actions to carry their maximum capacity of energy and force.

Tae Kwon Do Training

All basic standing, walking, and turning techniques in tae kwon do are taught by the instructor (the master) to a group, where the degree of difficulty depends on the experience of the participating students. A more experienced student will, of course, practice more advanced exercises; but the basics remain the same for students and master alike. Even a master practitioner will practice daily the same hitting techniques that a student is introduced to and is learning in his first lesson. It is, therefore, not *what* a student does that separates the beginner from the experienced student but *how* he does it!

The three fundamental categories of tae kwon do techniques—poomse, kyukpa and gyoroogi—are presented here in more detail.

Poomse (Formal Exercises)

Poomse exercises are mandatory, and, as in other sports, the different techniques are performed and judged in competition.

Poomse includes all attack and defense techniques. The degree of difficulty increases as the student moves to the next-higher poomse form. The sequence of movements is predetermined and is a means for the student to perfect techniques against his *imaginary opponent(s)*—one or more. The movements serve as an opportunity for the student to practice the different offensive and defensive techniques without the chance of injuries. The individual, compulsory exercises are performed in a prearranged H pattern.

Throughout the sequences a student is confronted with different situations and fights his imaginary opponents with systematic and practical actions. The student practices these techniques in predetermined, continuous sequences in which every movement is performed rhythmically with power and concentration, while maintaining balance throughout the exercise.

The extensive and specially designed exercises (stretching the tendons of the hips, legs, and feet) that precede the actual practice are a means of preparing the body for the more demanding movements by warming up the muscles, slowly activating the circulatory system, and strengthening the heart.

There are two specific exercise forms designed for the student (*gup* level or class):

- *pal-gwe*—1 to 8 *chang*
- *tae-kook*—1 to 8 *chang*

A master (*dan* or degree level) must know and perform the following compulsory exercises:

- *koryo* (Korea)
- *kum-kang* (diamond)
- *tae-book* (mountain—symbol of the country)
- *pyongwon* (plain)
- *shipjin* (ten)
- *jitae* (earth)
- *chonkwon* (heaven)
- *hansoo* (water)
- *ilyo* (unity)

In tae kwon do the human body is generally divided into three parts:

- *Eolgul* (face): from the top of the head to the collar bone,
- *Momtong* (trunk): from the collar bone to the navel,
- *Ahre* (lower body): from the navel on down.

Particularly during training, these divisions are of special importance for different offensive and defensive techniques. Particular training targets are used:

- *Eolgul: injung* (tip of the nose),
- *Momtong: myongchi* (solar plexus),
- *Ahre: danjon* (diaphragm, about two inches [5cm] below the navel).

Kyukpa (Breaking Technique)

Kyukpa is the discipline that we in the West are most familiar with and that many, mistakenly, believe represents the totality of tae kwon do. In reality, breaking an object is the least practiced part of it. Very seldom is it performed in isolation, but is, rather, part of a whole movement form. If a student has not acquired the skill to perform this test successfully during his basic training, his techniques are not yet sufficiently developed. Any attempt to do them too early—such as trying to compensate for a lack of skill with too much force—often results in painful injuries.

But what is that skill? In a way it is the technique that an athlete has practiced and perfected; but such practice has also given the student a kind of protective "layer" at those points on the arms and legs that are the target of hits and kicks. Any part of the body, any bone, ordinarily, would be too weak to withstand the impact when confronted with a solid brick. It is only the force of a determined mind and will—which together are the true source of such energy—that makes it possible for a human being to perform such a feat.

Gyoroogi (Sparring)

The techniques that a student has learned during the basic training are now tested during sparring competition. All exercises done separately and with breaks in between now become fluid movements, and the imaginary opponent that he or she has fought against is now replaced by a real opponent. Freestyle (jayu gyorooki) competitions are judged by the degree to which a student is in command of the technique that he encounters under difficult, real-life situations.

A competition with full contact requires from the athlete extraordinary skill, superior conditioning, lightning-fast reaction, self discipline (being tough on himself), and great courage.

Tae kwon do is a sport that makes great physical and psychological demands but none so difficult that every healthy person cannot achieve success.

What Is "Do"?

Since tae kwon do is a sport whose training requires the development not merely of athletic skills but also of a mental state that plays a vital role, a separate discussion of "do" is in order.

"Do" is the *way*, the *foundation*, the *lesson*, the open and unbiased subjective mind—a very basic attitude.

- The *way* is the meaning of life, meaning a method of study and training for the mind and the body that is practiced in daily life.
- The *foundation* is the forming of moral thinking (courteousness), courage and patience, willpower, fairness, humanity, self-discipline, concentration, motivation, and self-control.
- The *lesson* is a system that has at its goal a congruent development of the body as well as morality. This extends to physical education and training, including the psychological aspects: gaining wisdom and the training of mental capacities.

Attitude in Tae Kwon Do

If tae kwon do techniques are mastered and used properly, "do" serves:

- to perfect the *character* (*Dok*) through moral teachings (such as courteousness, humility, and honor),
- to teach *generosity* (*In*)—the physical and mental mastery of the ego (such as perseverance, self-control, patience, and fairness),
- to teach the *art* (*Ye*) of strengthening the body and the mind through the high art of self-defense.

In order to guide the body's physical energy in the proper direction, it is imperative that all participants practice regularly, in a disciplined way, while adhering to all rules of training.

> The highest goal of tae kwon do training is not to act thoughtlessly but to train one's personal attitude through discipline and body control.

Without adherence to these goals, tae kwon do can be a very dangerous, even brutal sport. Through carefully controlled systematic training, the functions of certain parts of the body—such as the hands and feet—can be changed in such a way that they can turn into something resembling a knife, a hammer, or a spear. Bringing about such changes depends on continuous training, on being patient, and on perseverance, as well as possessing the attitude and the ability to focus every ounce of energy on one specific point.

> Regular, consistent training makes it possible—on the one hand—to increase one's energy and—on the other—to use one's physical power effectively.

Practicing tae kwon do strengthens the physical body, making it supple, flexible, and strong. In addition to gaining a sense of physical well-being, participants also notice a change towards a more positive mental attitude—indeed, it seems as if there is an internal process working, which, on the surface, appears to be in stark contrast to this rather tough, self-defense method. Viewed in isolation, the acquired skills are indeed deadly instruments in the hands of an expert. But, in spite of this, the long-standing and rigorous teachings of tae kwon do have very seldom produced a bully or a thug.

> Tae kwon do develops body and mind.

The very first, basic level of training already increases the stamina and will-power of the student. Once this is realized, the student understands that only patience will allow him or her to progress. Being around the master and other, more experienced students teaches the student to be courteous and humble while, at the same time, it forces introspection and contemplation of his or her own behavior as well as that of others.

During competition the capacities for self-control, honorable conduct, and fairness are all strengthened. In addition, during the course of continued training the student begins to experience a sense of comradeship with fellow students. And from this experience the student develops characteristics such as integrity, loyalty, and readiness to help. The cumulative result of instilling these characteristics and their constant nurturing is what is meant by the term "do."

Dojang (Training Space)

The *dojang*—a space to gather for inner collection—refers to the room where young and old, male and female athletes come together—regardless of race or religion—in order to practice tae kwon do. In the dojang, or school, practitioners further and improve the art itself, as well as their own physical,

17

psychological, and aesthetic abilities. Prerequisite for reaching that goal is guidance by an instructor who is well schooled mentally as well as physically.

The tae kwon do instructor—*sabom,* or master—through his own authority creates an atmosphere in which a student can distance himself from mundanity and thereby effectively concentrate on the training before him.

Kyong-ye (Paying Respect)

Every tae kwon do athlete should not only follow all the rules and guidelines, but should also—during and away from training—adhere to certain formalities that they have been taught. Showing respect towards a participant who has a higher rank is one of the most important. The Korean greeting *kyong-ye* is a combination of two words:

> *kyong:* esteem, respect
> *ye:* courteousness, etiquette

To show respect, opponents bow while looking straight ahead at each other.

During training: Before and after each training session the participant with the highest rank (he stands to the left of the trainer) gives the command *"Cha-ryot sabom nim ke kyong-ye."* This is followed by the students simultaneously bowing to the trainer.

Practicing with a partner and during competition: Here, as a form of greeting, the trainer or the official gives the command *"Cha-ryot, kyong-ye."*

Kihop (Concentrated Power)

The Korean word *kihop* is a combination of two words:

> *ki:* mental and physical power, bioenergy
> *hop:* focusing on one specific point

How Does Kihop Come About?

In order to combine mental and physical power with the techniques, the practitioner puts his whole concentration on one specific point, holds his breath deep in the center of his body, and expels the air at the moment of attack with a loud, short outburst, *"Yat."* It is important to distinguish between the following:

- *Poomse*: here we have one or two different kinds of kihops that require a special form of concentration. Special attention is given to both during each training and during tests.
- *Han-bon gyoroogi* (practicing compulsory sparring with a partner): here we also distinguish between attacker and defender. The kihop of the attacker is a signal for the defender to prepare to counterattack; this is followed by the kihop of the defender, signaling his counterattack.
- *Jayu gyoroogi* (freestyle sparring): during competition, a participant wants to intimidate his opponent while at the same time focusing on his target.

The following table is an attempt to give the reader a better overall view of tae kwon do. These techniques are discussed in more detail in this and the following chapters. The actual instructions of the individual movements of the poomse pal-gwe and tae-kook 1 to 8 chang, koryo, kum-kang as well as tae-book are detailed in text and illustrations in the practice sections in the second half of the book.

Overview of Tae Kwon Do Techniques

Sogi	– Stance	Page 19
Maggi	– Block, defense	Page 23
Konggyokki	– Attacking techniques	Page 26
☐ Ji-ru-gi	☐ Fist punch	
☐ Chi-ru-gi	☐ Fingertip thrust	
☐ Chi-gi	☐ Punch	
☐ Cha-gi	☐ Kick	
Poomse	– Combinations of basic movements (forms) against an imaginary opponent	Pages 31–45 on
Han-bon gyoroogi	– Practice with a partner	Page 32
Baal-cha-gi	– Stepping technique	Page 35
Hosinsool	– The art of self-defense	Page 38
Kyukpa	– Breaking technique	Page 40

Sogi (Stance)

The different stances a practitioner assumes form the basis for all tae kwon do techniques. Properly performed, they will—first and foremost—provide stability and excellent balance, something that is important for all athletic activities, but particularly so for tae kwon do. Some positions are simply used to prepare the student for a practice session or before actual competition; others are assumed only for very short moments as preparation for performing a specific technique; whereas others are part of a general fighting stance.

The upper part of the body always remains upright. Leaning to either side, forward or backwards may lead to the loss of balance, putting the practitioner at a disadvantage.

From the moment a student assumes a stance he should continually change between tension and relaxation. If the body remains relaxed throughout, the techniques used would be too weak; but constant tension tires the body, and the techniques used would be carried out too slowly.

Moa Sogi (Closed Stance)

The heels and big toes are touching in this first position.

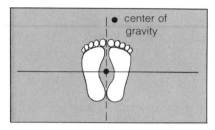

Cha-ryot Sogi (Attention Stance, V Stance)

Heels are in contact, feet pointing outwards at 22.5°; this position serves as preparation and aids concentration. The stance is assumed when tae kwon do athletes greet each other.

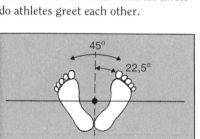

Kyorumse (Basic Fighting Stance)

From the Cha-ryot Sogi stance the right foot is moved back. The distance between feet is 1½ of shoulder width; knees are slightly bent, fists are held in front of the chest. The center of gravity is approximately at the middle of the body (see photo).

Kyorumse (basic fighting stance).

Pyong-hi Sogi (Ready Stance)

Feet are placed one foot length apart and slightly turned outside (22.5°); knees are locked.

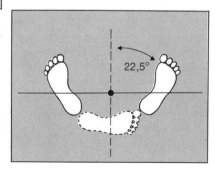

Naranhi Sogi (Open Parallel Stance)

Feet are parallel to each other, one foot-width apart; a typical preparatory stance. Another term is *junbi sogi*.

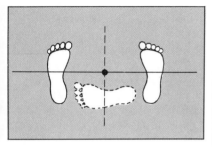

Juchoom Sogi (Horseback Stance)

Feet are securely set parallel to each other, with approximately two foot-widths apart; knees are slightly bent (the angle between thigh and lower leg is approximately 135°); the upper body is straight; body weight is distributed equally upon both legs.

Juchoomse is the assumption of the horseback stance.

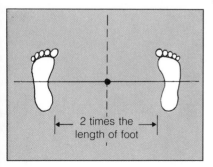

2 times the length of foot

Ahp-gubi Sogi (Forward Stance)

Both feet are planted securely on the ground; toes point straight ahead. The back foot may be turned approximately 22.5° to the outside. The back leg is straight, the front leg slightly bent. The upper body is straight, the weight of the body centered to the front.

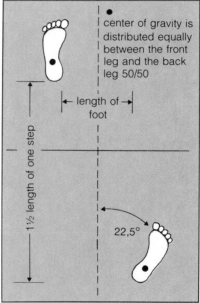

center of gravity is distributed equally between the front leg and the back leg 50/50

← length of → foot

1½ length of one step

22,5°

Ahp Sogi (Walking Stance)

When taking a normal step forward, the weight of the body is shifting slightly to the front foot. Remain in that position (*ahp sogi*). The back foot is pointing to the outside at a 22.5° angle (see diagram on the following page).

21

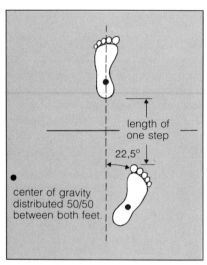

length of
one step

22,5°

center of gravity
distributed 50/50
between both feet.

Ahp sogi
(walking stance).

outside. The knee of the back leg is bent so that the toes are positioned beneath it. The upper body is straight and slightly to the side. Almost all of the body weight is on the back foot.

Poom Sogi (Tiger Stance)

Beginning with the cha-ryot sogi, one foot is placed forward by one foot-length. The heel of the front foot is lifted until only the toes are in touch with the ground. The knee of the back leg is bent, causing the body to move lower to the ground. Almost all of the body weight is on the back leg.

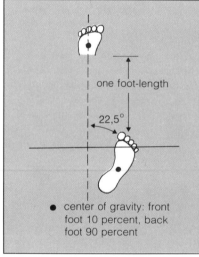

one foot-length

22,5°

center of gravity: front
foot 10 percent, back
foot 90 percent

Dwi-gubi Sogi (Back Stance)

Both feet are planted firmly on the ground. The front foot is pointing forward, the back foot is turned 90° to the

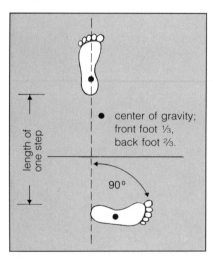

center of gravity;
front foot ⅓,
back foot ⅔.

length of
one step

90°

Hakdari Sogi (Crane Stance)

This stance is taken in preparation for a kick. The supporting foot is planted securely on the ground with the leg slightly bent. The foot of one leg is lifted up to the knee of the other.

Koa Sogi (Twisted Stance)

Koa sogi is a stance assumed typically for a side or forward movement. Legs are crossed. The foot of the supporting leg is planted solidly on the ground; at first only the ball of the foot touches the ground. Both knees are slightly bent. The upper body is straight, eyes are looking in the direction of the attack. There are two versions: the supporting foot is in front for *ahp-koa sogi* (moving to the side); the supporting foot is in back for *dwi-koa sogi* (forward movement).

Hakdari sogi (crane stance).

Koa sogi (twisted stance).

Maggi (Blocking, Defense)

Defensive techniques are meant to protect a fighter from being hit while preparing him for making a counterattack. During training, we distinguish between two types of blocking techniques:

- basic defense
- defense during competition

Basic defense that is taught at the beginner's level (just as with poomse combinations) includes all those defensive forms that a tae kwon do practitioner should be able to use to the optimum at any time.

23

Those defensive techniques used during competition are economically abbreviated to a minimum sequence, since the participant seldom has time for sweeping movements. A fighter defends himself from a protective position. Most blocking techniques are based on the principle of deflection. This means in practical terms that a rapidly moving mass, like a fist, is not stopped directly, but rather the direction of its travel is deflected.

Ahre Maggi (Low Block)

During basic training, ahre maggi starts at the vertical line of the opposite shoulder at shoulder height; the back of the fist is pointing up. The other arm (back of the fist also up) crosses over the blocking arm and is—at the same time and while the blocking action is carried out—pulled back to its original position from an outstretched position. The movement of the blocking arm ends about 10 inches (25cm) above the front knee, while the arm in its final phase is slightly bent. The shoulder is pushed forward slightly.

Defense is carried out with the outside lower arm. The position of the fist of the blocking arm is at about the middle of the body.

Momtong Maggi (Body Block)

This technique consists of many forms, differing in the way the hands are held and what type of defense is carried out. The standard form is momtong bakkat maggi (see photo on opposite page). An attack is defended against with either the inside or the outside of the lower arm—most often, however, with the outside arm.

Ahre maggi (low block).   Yop maggi (side block).   An maggi (inside block).

Bakkat maggi (outside block).   Eolgul maggi (face block).   Son-nal maggi (knife-hand block).

Momtong Yop Maggi (Side Body Block)

This block starts on the opposite hip. The fist of the blocking arm is turned up and the other arm is crossed over. The blocking arm goes past the outside arm—which is moved back, fist towards the hip—and is turned up just before reaching the end point. Increase speed and exertion to their maximum during the last third of the total movement. The arm is bent at the elbow by about 90 degrees.

Momtong An Maggi (Inside Body Block)

Here the defensive movement is carried out from the outside to the inside with the outside forearm (bakkat palmock) in front of the body. Start at the side of the body and bring the arm—hand in a fist—forward. Just prior to reaching the middle of the body the forearm is turned to the inside.

Momtong Bakkat Maggi (Outside Body Block)

Here the attack is defended against with the outside of the forearm (bakkat palmok) away from the body to the outside.

Eolgul Maggi (Face Block)

The arm blocking the attack—during practice—moves upwards directly from the hip, across the other arm, and at the last moment is turned up. Use maximum speed and exertion during the last third of the movement.

25

Hecho maggi (spreading block).

Son-nal Maggi (Knife-hand Block)

An attack is defended against with the edge of the hand moving in front of and from the right or left side of the body. The hand turns to the outside with the edge turned towards the target; the other hand (palm turned up) is held about an inch or so (3cm) in front of the solar plexus. (See photo on previous page.)

Hecho Maggi (Spreading Block)

Both arms are angled in front of the chest, with the back of the fists pointing outward. Then the arms are moved from the side forward, with the outside of the arms pointing outward. When the final phase is reached, both fists are opposite their respective shoulder. The arms are bent by about 90 degrees and elbows are moved slightly away from the body.

Additional Defense Techniques

Nullo maggi	– Downward block with ball of hand
Han sonnal maggi	– Blocking with the edge of hand
Otgoro maggi	– Double-fist cross block
Otgoro-ahre maggi	– Low double-fist cross block
Otgoro-eolgul maggi	– High cross block
Guduro maggi	– Double-hand block with support
Guduro-ahre maggi	– Low block with support
Guduro-momtong maggi	– Body block with support
Guduro-eolgul maggi	– Face block with support

Konggyokki (Attacking Techniques)

Attacking techniques are used in specific situations. Some may cause a person to collapse due to the interruption of blood flow; others, used in defense, may cause pain even though they are directed against less vulnerable parts of the body. And others can lead to serious internal or external injuries, some of which may be life-threatening.

The techniques are divided into hand/arm techniques and feet/leg techniques:

- *ji-ru-gi*: punch with fist
- *chi-ru-gi*: thrust with fingertips

Baro ji-ru-gi (walking punch).

Bandae ji-ru-gi (reverse punch).

- *chi-gi*: strike, hit with hand
- *cha-gi*: kick, hit with foot

Punching and thrusting carried out with the hands are the most effective techniques for an attack. Strike and kick techniques are a little slower but just as effective. The slowest are the kick techniques, but they make up for slowness by creating the greatest force.

Hand/Arm Techniques

Ji-ru-gi (Body Punch)

Ji-ru-gi means punching with the fist from the hips.

A tight fist hitting the target must always be pushed forward from the hips with great speed. Since the distance that the fist has to travel must be (or should be) as short as possible, its speed can be greatly increased by a 180-degree turn—meaning the back of the fist is moved down before it is pushed forward from the hip area.

As·the fist that does the punching is set in motion, the other hand is moving back while also being turned (making a counter-turn in the opposite direction).

Baro Ji-ru-gi (Walking Punch)

The punch is carried out with the fist on the opposite side of the body from where the weight is carried.

Bandae Ji-ru-gi (Reverse Punch)

Here the punching technique is to be carried out with the fist that is on the side where the weight of the body is carried.

Sonnal chi-gi (knife-hand strike).   Ahp cha-gi (front kick).   Dolryo cha-gi (round kick).

Sonnal Chi-gi (Knife-hand Strike)

The "knife hand" is formed by stretching out the fingers and turning the thumb under the palm. The point hitting the target is the edge of the hand between the little finger and the wrist.

Feet/Leg Techniques

Ahp Cha-gi (Front Kick)

Here the leg that is doing the kicking must be as close as possible to the supporting leg. The supporting leg is usually turned 60 degrees to the outside.

The knee of the kicking leg is pulled up as high as possible in preparation as it is pulled towards the body, and then—while kicking—the leg straightens out again. The target must be hit with the ball of the foot, meaning that the toes at the moment of impact are pulled back towards the body.

Dolryo Cha-gi (Round Kick)

The knee and thigh of the leg doing the kicking are lifted off the ground by bending the hips. The lower leg stretches forward with a snapping movement; at the same time, the supporting leg is rotated about 90 to 120 degrees.

During a fight the opponent is hit with the back of the foot; in a breaking test (kyukpa) the ball of the foot is used.

Dolryo cha-gi is the most frequently used technique during competition. It is a very effective technique, in which the target is either the body or the face of the opponent.

Yop Cha-gi (Side Kick)

The knee and thigh are lifted by bending at the hips. The force of the kick is amplified by turning the body towards the target. The foot and toes are flexed. The edge of the foot is held parallel to the ground and the knee of the kicking leg must be lower than the heel.

Yop cha-gı (side kick).

Dwi cha-gi (back kick).

When carried out correctly, the kicking leg will be completely straight after the impact.

Dwi Cha-gi (Back Kick)

The supporting leg is rotated by 180 degrees to the back. The kicking leg moves closely past the supporting leg, and the opponent is hit with the edge of the sole of the foot. The knee of the kicking leg must be as low as possible until the leg straightens out and the muscles are tensed.

Dwi-dolryo Cha-gi (Backward Turning Kick)

The supporting leg becomes the axis for a 180- or 360-degree rotation. The speed of the kicking leg is increased by the body's rotation along its vertical axis. The target is hit with the heel or the entire sole of the foot.

If the kicking leg is kept completely straight, the increase in speed is ac-

complished solely by the rotation of the body. If, however, the lower leg is bent just prior to impact, the speed will increase even more; the force at the moment of impact is much greater, perhaps double. The target is the face of the opponent.

Dwi-dolryo cha-gi (backward turning kick)

Basic Skills

Overview of Attacking Techniques

Ji-ru-gi (Punching Technique)
Baro ji-ru-gi — Walking punch
Bandae ji-ru-gi — Reverse punch
Yop ji-ru-gi — Side punch
Dolryo ji-ru-gi — Round punch
Naeryo ji-ru-gi — Downward punch
Chi ji-ru-gi — Uppercut punch
Sewo ji-ru-gi — Vertical punch
Jechyo ji-ru-gi — Punch with turned fist

Chi-ru-gi (Thrusting Technique)
Pyon-sonkut sewo chi-ru-gi — Vertical spear-hand fingertip thrust
Pyon-sonkut opo chi-ru-gi — Horizontal thrust
Pyon-sonkut jechyo chi-ru-gi — Turned-palm thrust
Gawi-sonkut chi-ru-gi — Scissor-hand thrust

Chi-gi (Striking Technique)
An chi-gi — Strike to the inside
Ahp chi-gi — Front strike
Bakkat chi-gi — Strike to the outside
Naeryo chi-gi — Downward strike
Eolgul chi-gi — Upward strike
for instance, with Palkoop — Elbow
                  Joomok — Fist
                  Moo-rup — Knee

Cha-gi (Kicking Technique)
Ahp cha-gi — Front kick
Yop cha-gi — Side kick
Dolryo cha-gi — Round kick
for instance: Bandae cha-gi — Reverse kick, mix of ahp and dolryo cha-gi
            Baal-dung dolryo cha-gi — Dolryo with instep
            Bakkat dolryo cha-gi — Outside round kick
            Dwi-dolryo cha-gi — Backward turning kick
            (Mom dolryo cha-gi)
Huryo cha-gi (ahn) — Wheel kick (inside)
for instance: Bakkat huryo cha-gi — Kick to the outside
Milo cha-gi — Push
for instance: Ahp-milo cha-gi — Push forward
            Yop-milo cha-gi — Push sideways
Naeryo cha-gi — Downward kick
Twi-o cha-gi — Jumping kick
for instance: Twi — Ahp cha-gi jump kick
            Twi-o yop cha-gi — Yop cha-gi jump kick
            Twi-o dolryo cha-gi — Dolryo cha-gi jump kick
            Twi-o dwi-dolryo cha-gi — Dwi-dolryo cha-gi jump kick

Gawi cha-gi	– Scissor jump kick
Modum-baal cha-gi	– Double-foot kick
for instance: Modum-baal ahp cha-gi	– Forward double-foot kick
Modum-baal yop cha-gi	– Backward double-foot kick
Dubaal dang-song	– Jumping double-foot kick

Poom & Poomse

Forms and Combinations of Different Movements Against an Imaginary Opponent

A considerable portion of this book is dedicated to poomse (pages 45–on). As an addition to this section on tech-niques, a table is presented below list-ing some of the typical sequences of movements and hand and arm posi-tions that are mentioned again in the section dealing with their perfor-mance. Also noted are the exact places where the movements occur within the individual poomse combinations.

Important Poom Movements from Different Poomse Forms

Bo-joomok	Tea-kook 7 chang (11)
Dolcho-gawi	Scissor
for instance: Jagun dolcho-gawi	Pal-gwe 8 chang (16, 22)
Kun dolcho-gawi	Kum-kang (9, 10, 16, 17, 19, 20, 26, 27)
Dwi chi-gi	Pal-gwe 8 chang (31)
Dwi ji-ru-gi	Pal-gwe 8 chang (34, 35)
Gawi maggi	Pal-gwe 5 chang (1, 10, 24); tea-kook 7 chang (12, 13)
Gyop-son	Pal-gwe 8 chang (32)
Jebipum mok chi-gi	Pal-gwe 6 chang (6); tea-kook 4 chang (5, 13); tea-book (5)
Jebipum tok chi-gi	Pal-gwe 6 chang (15)
Kum-kang maggi	Kum-kang (8, 15, 18, 25)
Kum-kang momtong maggi	Pal-gwe 4 chang (1, 4, 11, 14); tae-book (9, 14)
Monge paegi	Pushing off: pal-gwe 8 (33)
Owen-santul maggi	Pal-gwe 7 chang (21); tea-kook 8 chang (5, 7)
Pyojok chi-gi	Pal-gwe 7 chang (20); tae-kook 7 chang (21, 23); koryo (26)
Pyojok ji-ru-gi	Koryo (17, 22)
Santul maggi	Kum-kang (11, 14, 21, 24)

Technique Combinations

Combinations of Basic Techniques

As soon as one has mastered the basic skills sufficiently, the tae kwon do student may start combining several different techniques during practice (see table below). This would serve as preparation for practicing the formal exercises of pal-gwe, tae-kook, and poomse, such as combining ahp cha-gi (front kick) with yop cha-gi (side kick). During the course of a training session:

- When doing ahp gubi sogi (forward stance), you practice balance;
- When doing kyorumse (basic fighting stance), you practice for actual competition.

Han-bon Gyoroogi (Practicing Compulsory Sparring with a Partner)

Important Criteria for Han-bon Gyoroogi

- Mental requirements: focus and concentration
- Movements: exactness in attack and defense; proper distance (adjustment of distance)
- Kihop: controlled breathing; shouting to mobilize internal power (ki) and concentration as the signal for attack and defense
- Power: proper amount of force (strong/subtle)
- Body stretching: for a flexible body
- Nimbleness: a special skill

Gibon-dong Jakse (Combinations of Basic Techniques)		
Techniques	Stance	
	forward	backward
1. Ahre maggi	Ahp-gubi	Ahp sogi
2. Momtong bandae ji-ru-gi	Ahp-gubi	Ahp sogi
3. Momtong yop maggi	Dwi gubi	
Momtong bakkat		Ahp-gubi
4. Momtong maggi	Ahp-gubi	
Momtong an maggi		Ahp sogi
5. Ahp cha-gi	Ahp-gubi	Kyorumse
6. Son-nal chi-gi	Ahp-gubi	
Son-nal an chi-gi		Ahp sogi
7. Eolgul maggi	Ahp-gubi	Ahp sogi
8. Yop cha-gi	Ahp-gubi	Kyorumse
9. Son-nal momtong maggi	Dwi gubi	Dwi gubi
10. Momtong baro ji-ru-gi	Ahp-gubi	Ahp sogi

Note:
Sijak: At the beginning of junbi sogi, start out by stepping back with the right foot. Finish with ahp sogi to ahp-gubi; then momtong ji-ru-gi (kihop).
Guman: Step back again with the right foot (junbi sogi).

Basic Principles

1. Partners stand facing each other, about 3ft (1m) apart.
2. At the start, and after the finish, both bow to each other.
3. Partners maintain eye contact throughout the practice.
4. Partners alternate between attack and defense.
5. The blocking movement—using the correct defensive action—is initiated immediately before the attacking action reaches a critical part of the body.
6. When evading an attack, make sure that the distance to the partner is such that you can launch into a counterattack in one movement.
7. The counterattack should follow immediately after the last defensive movement.
8. Both partners are using only those techniques that they have have been taught and that are part of their training exercises.
9. Right- and left-oriented attack and defense techniques should be used with equal frequency.

Hand Techniques

Exercise

Junbi sogi (attention stance)
Konggyokki (attacking techniques)
Banggoki (blocking techniques)

Movements

for 1/2/3: **Juchoom sogi**
for 4/5/6: **Dwi-gubi**; ⅔ back, ⅓ forward
for 7/8/9: **Ahp-gubi**; 1 step back, ½ step forward
for 10/11/12: **Ahp sogi**; 1 step forward

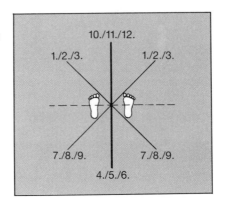

Explanation

Owen: left
Orun: right
  a: ahp-gubi
aps: ahp sogi
  d: dwi-gubi
  j: juchoom sogi

A student should master all techniques for the left and right side. For simplicity's sake we are only demonstrating those for the right side.

33

Technique Combinations

Action

1. Owen son-nal (eolgul bakkat) maggi
   Orun momtong ji-ru-gi and owen momtong ji-ru-gi / j
2. Owen son-nal bakkat maggi
   Orun son-nal mok chi-gi / j
3. Owen son-nal bakkat maggi
   Orun momtong ji-ru-gi / J; and owen palkoop ahp chi-gi / a
4. Orun (palmok) eolgul an maggi / d
   Orun palkoop yop maggi and dung-joomok chi-gi / j
5. Orun eolgul an maggi / d
   Owen momtong baro ji-ru-gi and orun dung-joomok ahp chi-gi / a
6. Orun eolgul bakkat maggi / d
   Owen-orun palkoop dwi chi-gi / j
7. Owen son-nal eolgul bakkat maggi
   Orun eolgul baro ji-ru-gi / a; and owen son-nal momtong yop ji-ru-gi / d
8. Owen son-nal eolgul bakkat maggi
   Orun son-nal an chi-gi / a; and owen son-nal bakkat chi-gi / d
9. Owen son-nal eolgul bakkat maggi / a
   Orun son-nal dung an chi-gi / a; and owen son-nal dung momtong chi-gi / d
10. Owen son-nal eolgul bakkat maggi
    Orun ba-tang-son tok chi-gi and owen ba-tang-son tok chi-gi / aps
11. Owen son-nal eolgul bakkat maggi
    Orun agumson mok chi-gi and owen gawi-sonkut chi-ru-gi / aps
12. Otgoro-eolgul maggi and hecho maggi, sewo ji-ru-gi, and jechyo ji-ru-gi / aps

Feet/Leg Techniques

Practice Protocol

1. Students A and B stand facing each other, about 3ft (1m) apart.
2. Before and after each action they bow to each other.
3. The trainer first gives the command *cha-ryot* ("Stand at attention") and then *kyong-ye* ("Greetings").
4. The trainer gives the command to assume **kyorumse** (basic fighting stance) and **junbi** (step back with right foot into the preparation stance).
5. This is followed by the command *sijak* ("Begin to fight").
6. A (attacker): *Yat* shout (kihop) for his attack (directed to his partner).
   B (defender): *Yat* shout as an answer (ready to defend).

Example:

A carries out attack (for example, ahp cha-gi).

B answers with the corresponding defense action.

Note: Students should master all techniques for both the left and the right sides.

Action

1. Technique:	a)	evasive step with the right foot (rf), about 45 degrees back to the left / diagonal step.
	b)	ahp cha-gi with rf.
2. Technique:	a)	as in 1 a).
	b)	dolryo cha-gi with rf.
3. Technique:	a)	as in 1 a).
	b)	huryo cha-gi or naeryo cha-gi with rf.
4. Technique:	a)	as in 1 a).
	b)	yop cha-gi with left foot (lf).
5. Technique:	a)	as in 1 a).
	b)	dwi cha-gi with rf.
6. Technique:	a)	as in 1 a).
	b)	dwi-dolryo cha-gi with rf.
7. Technique:	a)	evasion tactic; pull the front foot towards the back foot.
	b)	at the same time, carry out dolryo cha-gi.
8. Technique:	a)	evasion tactic; with the front foot step behind the back foot about 30 degrees and immediately . . .
	b)	. . . carry out ahp-myolo cha-gi or naeryo cha-gi (sliding attack).
9. Technique:	a)	evasion by stepping back.
	b)	bakkat huryo cha-gi with starting step.
10. Technique:	a)	evasion by carrying out closing step—backwards.
	b)	yop cha-gi with closing step—forward (sliding attack).
11. Technique:	a)	as in 10 a).
	b)	dwi cha-gi (sliding attack).
12. Technique:	a)	as in 10 a).
	b)	Twi-o dwi dolryo cha-gi (sliding attack).

Note: Techniques 10, 11, and 12 should be practiced with both an open and closed side stance.

Baal-jit-ki (Stepping Techniques)

What Does "Stepping" Mean?

The so-called stepping techniques are critical in modern competition and are the foundation for every shift that the body is making. What is important here is that the center of gravity is shifted smoothly from one point to another. A student who has mastered the stepping techniques is said to be keeping his body in perfect balance.

When you are practicing the stepping techniques, it is important that the whole body, including the fist, does not tense up. In addition, the feet must be "sliding" as closely as possible over the floor to keep the body in balance. Stepping also plays a decisive role during defense, attack, and when carrying out diversionary tactics.

Technique Combinations

Step-Training and What to Watch Out For

1. Practice by staying in one place.
2. Avoid jumping; stand relaxed on the balls of your feet.
3. Feet should not—under any circumstances—come together.
4. Practice techniques moving to the left *and* right.
5. Movements should be carried out quickly. Always pretend that you are fighting an imaginary opponent.

The **goal of the training** is to maximize your reaction responses by using the step techniques to maintain balance. Objectives in the training of stepping techniques are:

- coordination of movements,
- controlling distance and timing (for instance, stance and position of the opponent),
- quickness of movements and carrying out movements correctly,
- even rhythm of movements.

Weight Distribution Methods During Step-Training

- Intensive intervals: do exercises five to 10 times with 50 to 80 percent intensity.
- Quick movements: carry out the series of movements as fast as possible (explosive quality). After every series (consisting of five or six exercises) take a two- to five-minute break.
- Effective training: increase speed as well as duration for increased stamina.

Practicing Stepping Techniques

Description

A: Ahp cha-gi

D: Dolryo cha-gi

Dwi: Dwi cha-gi

N: Naeryo cha-gi

BH: Bakkat huryo cha-gi

AM: Ahp-myolo cha-gi

YM: Yop-myolo cha-gi

H: Huryo cha-gi

Action

1. **Naga (starting step):** A - D - Y- H - BH
   - from kyorumse either left foot (lf) forward or right foot (rf) back.
   - rf one step forward, then attack with lf.
   This stepping technique is particularly good when launching an attack.
2. **Dwi-dolla (backward turning step):** D - Y - H - AM
   - from kyorumse (as above).
   - step back 180 degrees with rf, then attack with lf.
3. **Bikyo (diagonal step):** A - D - M - H - N
   - as above.
   - side-step diagonally with back rf, and immediately attack with the same foot (rf).

4. **Mullo (back step)**: D - N - H - Y - Dwi
   - as above.
   - front foot moves back one step.
   - from this position both feet can be used for an attack.
5. **Moa (closing step)**: D - H - Dwi
   - from yop kyorumse or kyorumse.
   - Draw the back foot forward beside the front foot with legs together, and immediately attack with the front foot.
6. **Koa (cross step)**: D - H - Y
   - from yop kyorumse or kyorumse.
   - place the back foot in front of the front foot, and immediately attack with the front foot.
7. **Kullomoa (switch step)**: D - AM - N - Y - H
   - from kyorumse.
   - draw the front foot towards the back foot and, at the same time, use the back foot for attack.
8. **Dullo (step by lifting foot)**: D - AM - N - Y - H
   - as above.
   - stepping on one leg:
     a) pursue with front foot raised.
     b) pursue while back foot is raised and brought forward.

Countertechniques

What follows are samples of counter-techniques as they become necessary within the course of exercising.

Steps: sts = starting step
xs = cross step
ds = diagonal step
ss = switch step
bs = back step

Description

Stance: os = open stance
cs = closed stance

Kick/Leg: ff = front foot
bf = back foot

Punch/Hand: fh = front hand
bh = back hand

Sequence of Action							
Attacking Technique	Stance	Step	Kick/Leg Punch/Hand	Countertechnique	Step	Kick/Leg Punch/Hand	
1. Dolryo cha-gi	os		bf	Myolo cha-gi		ff	
			bf	Dwi cha-gi		bf	
			bf	Momtong ji-ru-gi	ds	fh	
	cs	xs	ff	Dwi dolryo or		bf	
				Dwi huryo cha-gi, respectively		bf	
		xs	ff	Naeryo cha-gi		ff	

Sequence of Action

Attacking Technique	Stance	Step	Kick/Leg Punch/Hand	Countertechnique	Step	Kick/Leg Punch/Hand
2. Ahp cha-gi	cs		bf	Dolryo cha-gi	ds	bf
			bf	Ahp cha-gi	ds	bf
			bf	Yop cha-gi	ds	ff
			bf	Naeryo or	ds	bf
				An huryo cha-gi	ds	bf
			bf	Dwi huryo cha-gi	ds	bf
			bf	Momtong ji-ru-gi	ds	bh
3. Yop cha-gi	os/cs	ss	ff	Naeryo or		bf
				An huryo cha-gi	ds	bf
	cs	ss	ff	Dwi dolryo cha-gi	xs	bf
	os	ss	ff	Ahp cha-gi	ds	bf
		ss	ff	Yop cha-gi	ds	ff
		ss	ff	Dolryo cha-gi	sts	bf
		ss	ff	Momtong ji-ru-gi	ds	bh
4. Dwi cha-gi	os		bf	Dolryo cha-gi	ds	bf
	cs		bf	Dolryo cha-gi	ss	bf
5. Dwi dolryo cha-gi	cs		bf	Ahp myolo	ds	bf
				Dolryo cha-gi	ds	bf
			bf	Dwi dolryo cha-gi	bs	bf
				Momtong ji-ru-ki	ds	bf
6. Momtong ji-ru-gi	os	sts	bh	Dwi cha-gi		bf
		sts	bh	Dwi dolryo cha-gi		bf

Hosinsool (The Art of Self-Defense)

Hosinsool requires a maximum amount of attention, decisiveness, quickness, ability to react, and intuition. In addition, participants need to have full mastery of all techniques.

Attacks with a weapon require a great deal of caution—and more quickness and more decisiveness than attacks without a weapon. For the former, one ought not only practice the standard techniques but also, if only to acquire more confidence, practice with an opponent. This is the only way to prepare for a real-life confrontation with an armed opponent.

The one defending himself should try as much as possible to find an unprotected and vulnerable area of the opponent and hit that area quickly and effectively. The defensive moves chosen depend on the the type of attack. The defender's size in relation to that of the opponent also must be taken into consideration.

Criteria of Hosinsool

1. Attack and defense position.
2. Type of movement from the basic stance:

- evasion, defending through sliding, stepping, crossover, body turns, stepping-turns;
- turning in all directions.

Defending Against Attack—Being Grabbed

Take Hold of the Wrists
- with one hand
  - on the same side
  - on the opposite side
- with both hands
  - from the front
  - from the back
- with both hands around one hand
  - open
  - closed

Techniques
- hand forced up
- hand forced down
- hand forced to the side
- arm twisting
- press with fingers
- bend/twist hand
- hand pressing, etc

Defending Against Being Grabbed by the Lapels
- with one hand
- with both hands

Techniques
- twist/stretch movement
- hand twisted to the side

Defense Against Choking Attack

- with one hand
  - from the front
  - from behind
- with both hands
  - from the front
  - from behind
  - from the side

Techniques
- hand forced up
- hand forced down
- hand forced to the side
- arm twisting
- finger presses
- hand bending/ twisting
- hand pressing, etc.

Defense Against Gripping Attack

Body Is Held in a Clutch
- from the front
  - under the arms
  - over the arms

Techniques
- bending opponent's body backwards
- striking with the hammer-fist
- hitting the head
- twisting the neck

Body Clutch
- from behind
  - under the arms
  - on top of the arms

Techniques
- using leg as lever
- hit with knee
- hit/kick with heel, etc.

Grabbed Around the Neck
- from the front
- from behind

39

Techniques
- finger press
- arm used as lever
- break with the arm
- arm wrenching, etc.
- arm wrenching
- arm used as lever, etc.
- twisting the hand

Defense Against an Attack with a Knife or Club

- attack
  - from the front
  - from the outside
  - from the inside
- attack from behind

Techniques
- brushing with the hand
- breaking the arm

Kyukpa (Breaking Test)

Criteria for Kyukpa

1. Focus: increase mental concentration.
2. Judge: distance and angle to the target.
3. Power: coming from the hip.
4. *Kihop:* explosive internal power.
5. Dexterity: specific movement skills acquired through consistent training.

The breaking test, kyukpa.

Competition takes place within an 8m × 8m (26¼ft × 26¼ft) contest area enclosed by a 12m × 12m (39⅓ ft × 39⅓ft) competition area box. It is conducted according to established rules. Participants may use all techniques in accordance with regulations. The winner is decided by the referee, according to a point system based on successful hits (solid contact) using hands and feet.

The first official Tae Kwon Do World Championships were held at the Kukkiwon Arena in Seoul, Korea, on the 25th of May, 1973.

Requirements for Participants

1. Character: moral, ideological qualification, basic convictions, psychological characteristics necessary for competition.
2. Conditioning: energy, quickness, stamina.
3. Technical coordination: agility of movement, coordinating ability.
4. Tactics: tactical knowledge as well as technical/tactical ability (ability to observe, ability to think) and skill, concrete tactical ability, effectiveness of tactical maneuvers, behavior and action during competition.
- ability to observe the opponent, trainer, coach, rules of the competition, etc.
- ability to think (tactical thinking): mental process whereby the means to the end is subordinated to the prevailing situation of the fight.

Developing the ability to think is one of the most important factors in tactical/technical training.

Positions Assumed in Competition

1. **Kyorumse (Basic Fighting Stance)**
- body turned slightly sideways
- distance between legs: 1½ shoulder-width

2. **Ahp Kyorumse (Facing Forward)**
- body facing straight forward
- distance between legs: 1 shoulder-width

3. **Natchumse (Low Position)**
- body positioned sideways, upper body bent forward
- distance between legs: 1½ shoulder-width

4. **Yop Kyorumse (Side Position)**
- body positioned sideways
- distance between legs: approximately 1½ shoulder-width

Tips
- Practice difficult positions often.
- The distance between the legs should always be slightly wider than the shoulders.
- Knees should always be slightly bent and the student should bounce lightly with the lower legs (knees and heels) throughout the exercise.
- Fists should be held in front of the chest for protection.
- Body weight must be centered on the balls of the feet.

41

Competition

Suggestions for Competitors

Warm-Up

Warming up before a competition (as well as before training) prepares and stimulates the circulatory system. Physiological/chemical processes initiate an increase in energy availability. These chemical processes warm up the musculature and prepare the participants psychologically for the competition ahead.

Warm-up Program

1. exercises such as running and jumping
2. warm-up exercises
3. gentle stretching
4. exercises requiring the gentle use of force

Tips on Methods

1. The duration of a warm-up program should be about 10 to 20 minutes, allowing the body to loosen up and reflexes to sharpen.
2. Start out gently and slowly increase the intensity of exercises. Do 3 to 5 exercises with 10 to 15 repetitions for each.
3. Goal of the warm-up: to increase flexibility—generally or in specific areas such as arms and shoulders, bending side-to-side, hips and legs, joints used for jumping.

Self-Massage

Self-massage is an excellent means to increase performance—even if it is not nearly as effective as receiving a massage from somebody else. However, one of the advantages of self-massage is that it can be done without outside help and that areas where muscles are particularly sensitive can be attended to more intensely (leg massage, massage of the hitting arm). Of course, self-massage can only be a partial massage.

When Is a Massage Not Appropriate?
In the case of fresh injuries, when inflammations are present, in the presence of skin disorders, and in the area of various veins, massage should be avoided.

Tips to Prevent Injuries

- Maintain the best possible nutrition during the days prior to a competition.
- Always do warm-up exercises before the start of the competition.
- Make sure that you receive appropriate psychological support from the trainers and are advised of the opponent's tactical expertise.
- Knowing and upholding all rules of the competition is a must.
- The fundamental principle of training is to instill in the student a sense of fairness and sportsman-like conduct—this will avoid any possibility of ugly scenes during a bout.

Points to Remember During Competition

1. Always conduct a fair and active fight (displaying technical and physiological initiative).
2. Avoid warnings and penalty points (pay attention to the rules and regulations of the competition).
3. Follow the instructions from your trainer (strategic coordination).
4. Study the opponent as soon as possible (observing his techniques and tactics).
5. Change your own techniques, steps, and evasive maneuvers often (changing your tactics).
6. Sensibly adjust how you use your energy—make it last over all three rounds.
7. Some basic tips:
   - during attack:
     → judging (distances, target, what kind of techniques to use)
     → starting (two or more combinations of actions)
     → protecting
   - during counterattack:
     → protection through evasion
     → starting (action)
     → protection

- in case of an attack:
  → **important** to initiate during a forward movement, not while at a standstill

Situations Demanding Tactical Response

- fighting an opponent who is taller
- fighting an opponent who is smaller
- fighting an opponent who tends to counter after an evastive movement
- fighting an opponent who generally blocks an attack by raising the front leg
- fighting an opponent who only tries to counter
- fighting an opponent who reacts continuously with wild attacks
- fighting an opponent who generally keeps his arms in front of the body as a defense but makes no evasive moves
- deciding what to do when in a hold
- deciding what to do when there is an opportunity for attack
- knowing what to do after the command *Kalyeo* ("Break") has been given by the referee
- receiving a warning or a point deduction

Poomse

Overview

Poomse		Number of Poom	Number of Dong-jak	Target of Kihop	Diagram from the point of view of the opponent
PAL-GWE	1 Chang	20	20	8, 16	
	2 Chang	20	26	8, 16	
	3 Chang	22	22	8, 22	
	4 Chang	24	28	10, 20	
	5 Chang	35	39	13, 27	
	6 Chang	19	29	7, 16	
	7 Chang	23	29	17, 23	
	8 Chang	35	40	10, 35	
TAE-KOOK	1 Chang	18	20	18	
	2 Chang	18	23	18	
	3 Chang	20	34	20	
	4 Chang	20	29	20	
	5 Chang	20	32	20	
	6 Chang	19	31	12	
	7 Chang	25	33	25	
	8 Chang	27	38	3, 19	
KORYO		30	50	11, 30	
KUM-KANG		27	27	11, 21	
TAE-BOOK		26	40	8, 22	

Criteria for the performance of all poomse forms:

1. **Mental:** clarity of purpose and attitude
2. **Posture:** center of gravity, precise movement
3. **Force:** utilizing energy properly (application forceful/smooth) and speed (fast/slow)
4. **Kihop:** control breathing—shouting after having mobilized internal energy (Ki) and focused concentration
5. **Aesthetic:** rhythm of movements
6. **Dignity:** composure

What follow are descriptions and illustrations of all Pal-Gwe and Tae-Kook forms, as well as Koryo, Kum-Kang, and Tae-Book. A short introduction explains the meaning of each Poomse.

The individual sequences of movements always follow the basic outline of a certain diagram. Indications of the direction of the movements are always given as seen by the person who does the exercises.

B = Back   F = Front
R = Right (1+2+3)   L = Left (1+2+3)

Pal-Gwe

One of the oldest philosophical writings of east Asia is the *I Ching: Book of Changes* (in Korea, *Juyok*). At the center of this work are eight basic principles, the *pal-gwe*, that, in the way they interact, can be understood as being a mirror of all that takes place in the Universe.

The idea of *pal-gwe* embraces different symbols and includes all opposing concepts and images. They grow through the process of constant change as well as countless combinations and are in an endless state of development. This means that, for instance, a constant change takes place between heaven and earth, men and women, light and dark, goodness and evil, depending on how these eight phenomena come together, mingle, and separate again. All this is subject to a determined regularity. The world of *pal-gwe,* therefore, rests on the changes and interaction of different elements—it is a world of opposite poles.

These forms are meant to give the student an understanding of the basic principles of tae kwon do, which are characterized by contrast—change and coming together, conflict and harmony—thereby corresponding to the idea of *pal-gwe.*

Tae-Kook

Translated from the Chinese characters, *Tae* means greatness, and *Kook* means eternity. The combination of these two words makes it clear that here the philosophy of eastern Asia is very much present. Without form, without a beginning, and without an end, tae-kook represents the essence of all that is.

Eight basic Eastern principles are developed in tae-kook. They are represented by eight symbols and each one of them has a specific meaning in Chinese writing. In ancient times these symbols were a sign of power. And to this day four of them are found in the South Korean flag.

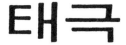

Koryo

Koryo is the name of one of the Southeast Asian dynasties (A.D. 918–1392). The name *Korea* was derived from the name of this kingdom.

The cultural heritage that has been passed on to the Korean people from that time is of great importance to them. It was during the Koryo Dynasty that for the first time printing was done with letters made from metal (1234)—in other words, almost 200 years before Johannes Gutenberg (1390–1468) invented printing with movable type in Germany. It was also during this time that the very famous Koryo ceramics were produced. In addition, the Korean people displayed an enormous amount of courage as they defended themselves successfully against attacks from Mongolia, whose armies were invading much of the then-known Eastern world.

The spiritual and mental strength of the people of the Kingdom of Koryo has found expression in the movement forms of tae kwon do and lead to the poomse koryo. Each action in this poomse expresses the strong conviction and the mental power that was particular to the peoples of Koryo as they stood against the Mongolian invaders.

Kum-Kang

The meaning of *kum-kang* originally was "too strong to be broken." In Buddhism *kum-kang* has a broader meaning: every emotional pain can be ended with a combination of wisdom and virtue.

The Korean people gave the name *kum-kang-san* to one of their most beautiful peninsulas. This area belongs to the tae-book mountain region. The hardest matter, the diamond, is called *kum-kang-sok.*

Along the same lines, tae kwon do names one of the movement forms

kum-kang. Kum-kang has mental power as its basis, while evoking the beauty of the Kum-kang Mountains and, at the same time, the hardness of diamond.

The form of this movement was modelled after the Chinese character for *mountain.* Accordingly, the sequence of movements should be performed with a strong but endlessly changing, majestic expression—similar to the image that a mountain conveys.

Tae-Book

A legend about the origin of ancient Korea describes, among other things, how the Tungusic tribes settled the region, founding the country—about 4300 years ago—at the Tae-book, today called Baek-doo, Mountain. This mountain is considered to be the most imposing and grand of the Korean peninsula and is considered to be a holy mountain. This is one explanation for the type of movements of the poomse form tae-book. The Tae-book Mountain is a symbol for Korea. For that reason the movements should not only be performed with precision and speed but also with strength and determination.

Poomse

Meanings of the Exercise Diagrams (Plan-view Sequence of Movements)

Pal-Gwe and Tae-Kook—1 to 8 Chang

1 (Il) Chang
The diagram for 1 chang symbolizes the heavens and light; the sequence of movements of the poomse are dedicated to them. The rain and the light of the sun—necessary for all that grows—both come from the heavens. The heavens, therefore, are the symbol of creation, the beginning of everything there is.

2 (Le) Chang
The diagram for 2 chang symbolizes cheerfulness and happiness. A person who is filled with happiness is a person possessing inner strength as well as maintaining and conveying to others a sense of calmness and balance.

3 (Sam) Chang
3 chang is symbolized by the sign of fire. Through intelligence, humans were able to tame fire. Fire gives warmth and light to us; it excites us and gives us hope and confidence; but it also awakens passion, fear, and panic in us.

4 (Sa) Chang
The symbol for 4 chang stands for thunder. Thunder and lightning strike fear into people; but thunder also creates energy.

Correspondingly, the principle of this poomse is to confront danger with calmness and courage in the form of powerful and focused (quick) movements.

5 (Oh) Chang
The symbol of the wind represents 5 chang. In spite of turning into storms, wind also has a positive meaning, because wind disperses seeds and scatters dark clouds. Wind symbolizes a force of destruction as well as the power to build.

6 (Yuk) Chang
The symbol of water characterizes 6 chang. Like water that always flows down, the movements here are fluid, flowing into one another. This image teaches us that difficulties and misfortune can be overcome if we proceed with self-confidence.

The movements that have been developed with this idea in mind follow the flow of water; individual parts are bridged by kicking action of the feet.

7 (Chil) Chang
The Chinese character expressing 7 chang symbolizes the highest point or, literally, the summit of the mountain. The diagram here is the mountain. A mountain is seemingly permanent and unmovable, and we human beings seek to emulate these characteristics by moving forward, if necessary, and staying still when that is called for. Moving forward and remaining still are both necessary when we want to achieve something.

8 (Pal) Chang

The eighth and last pal-gwe and tae-kook diagram symbolizes Earth, which is the source of all life. Everything arises from the Earth, receiving its nourishment and its energy. The creative power of the heavens is embodied in the Earth.

8 chang is the last form a student learns on the way to becoming a dan (degree-holding black belt). These basic forms are revisited and practiced again and again until they are polished to perfection.

Koryo

As described, the name for an early dynasty and kingdom in the region of Korea a thousand years ago was Koryo. The diagram corresponds to the Chinese character for *scholar/wise man.*

Kum-Kang

The diagram corresponds to the Chinese character for *mountain.*

Tae-Book

This diagram is modelled after the symbol for the founding of Korea at Tae-book Mountain, which is now known as Baek-doo. The bottom line symbolizes Earth, the upper line is heaven, and the vertical line is the person, representing the connection of all.

Training Recommendations

- Each poomse must stop where it began.
- Correct position and balance must be present at all times.
- Muscles should, depending on the movement carried out at the moment, be either flexed or relaxed.
- Each poomse should be performed with rhythm and elegance.
- Depending on the poomse, movements should be speeded up or slowed down appropriately.
- Master each poomse before moving on to the next.

Conduct During Training

- Before starting the exercises, meditate, warm up, and review what was taught previously.
- When performing the different movements, pay attention to proper breathing and *think,* don't just imitate.
- Bring techniques and mental concentration into balance.
- Maintain courtesy and humility towards others before and during exercises.
- Bow before the master (instructor) and the partner when entering and leaving the training area.
- Keep the dobok (uniform) always in good condition and make certain the ty (belt) is properly tied.
- Do not wear jewelry (rings, chains, etc.) during training (danger of injuries).

Pal-Gwe 1 Chang

	Body and Leg Movements	Stance	Hand Techniques
Junbi	Look in the direction F and step sideways with the left foot.	Naranhi sogi	Gibon junbi
1	Turn left and place left foot forward one step in the direction of L1.	Owen ahp-gubi	Ahre maggi
2	Place right foot one step towards L1.	Orun ahp-gubi	Momtong maggi
3	Turn body on the ball of right foot 180 degrees to the right and move right foot forwards in the direction of R1.	Orun ahp-gubi	Ahre maggi
4	Move left foot one step forward in the direction of R1.	Owen ahp-gubi	Momtong maggi
5	Turn on the ball of the right foot towards left, place left foot a step in the direction F.	Owen ahp-gubi	Ahre maggi
6	Move right foot one step forward in the direction F.	Owen dwi-gubi	Momtong yop maggi
7	Move left foot one step forward in the direction F.	Orun dwi-gubi	Momtong yop maggi
8	Move right foot one step forward in the direction of in the direction F.	Orun ahp-gubi	Momtong bandae ji-ru-gi (Kihop)
9	Turn to the left on your right foot—moving the left foot in the direction of R2.	Orun dwi-gubi	Son-nal momtong maggi
10	Move right foot one step forward in the direction of R2.	Owen dwi-gubi	Momtong maggi
11	Turn right 180 degrees on the ball of the left foot, and move the right foot forward in the direction of L2.	Owen dwi-gubi	Son-nal momtong maggi
12	Move the left foot one step forward in the direction of L2.	Owen dwi-gubi	Momtong maggi

Continued on following pages.

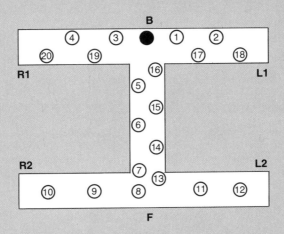

Pal-Gwe 1 Chang

	Body and Leg Movements	Stance	Hand Techniques
13	Turn left on the ball on the right foot, and move the left foot in the direction B.	Owen ahp-gubi	Ahre maggi
14	Move right foot one step forward in the direction B.	Orun ahp-gubi	Orun han-son-nal mok chi-gi
15	Move left foot one step forward in the direction B.	Owen ahp-gubi	Owen han-son-nal mok chi-gi
16	Move right foot one step forward in the direction B.	Orun ahp-gubi	Momtang bandae ji-ru-gi (Kihop)
17	Turn left on the ball of the right foot, and move the left foot in the direction of L1.	Owen ahp-gubi	Ahre maggi
18	Move the right foot one step in the direction of L1.	Orun ahp-gubi	Momtong maggi
19	Turn right 180 degrees on the ball of the left foot, and move the right foot in the direction of R1.	Orun ahp-gubi	Ahre maggi
20	Move the left foot one step forward in the direction of R1.	Owen ahp-gubi	Momtong maggi
Guman	Turn left on the ball of the right foot, and look in the direction F.	Naranhi sogi	Gibon junbi

Continued on following pages.

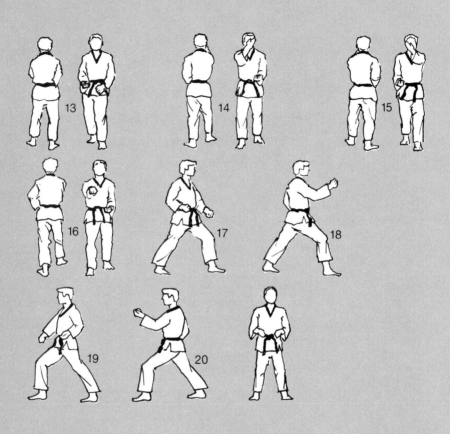

Pal-Gwe 2 Chang

	Body and Leg Movements	Stance	Hand Techniques
Junbi	Look in the direction F, and move the left foot to the side.	Naranhi sogi	Gibon junbi
1	Turn to your left foot, and move the left foot in the direction of B.	Owen ahp-gubi	Eolgul maggi
2	Kick with the right foot—ahp cha-gi—and then lower the foot in the direction of L1.	Orun ahp-gubi	Momtong bandae ji-ru-gi
3	Turn on the ball of your left foot 180 degrees to the right, and place the right foot forward in the direction of R1.	Orun ahp-gubi	Eolgul maggi
4	Kick with the left foot—ahp cha-gi—and then lower the foot in the direction of R1.	Owen ahp-gubi	Momtong bandae ji-ru-gi
5	Turn on the ball of your right foot to your left, and then lower the foot in the direction F.	Orun ahp-gubi	Son-nal ahre maggi
6	Move the right foot one step forward in the direction F.	Owen dwi-gubi	Son-nal momtong maggi
7	Move the left foot forward in the direction F.	Owen ahp-gubi	Eolgul maggi
8	Move the right foot forward one step in the direction F.	Orun ahp-gubi	Momtong bandae ji-ru-gi (Kihop)
9	Turn to your right on the ball of the right foot, and place the left foot forward in the direction F.	Owen ahp-gubi	Eolgul maggi
10	Kick with the right foot—ahp cha-gi—and then lower the foot to the ground in the direction of R2.	Orun ahp-gubi	Momtong bandae ji-ru-gi

Continued on following pages.

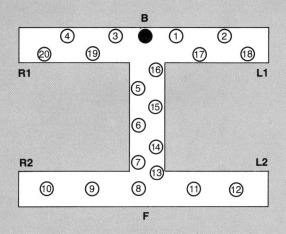

Pal-Gwe 2 Chang

	Body and Leg Movements	Stance	Hand Techniques
11	Turn 180 degrees to the right on the left foot, and move the right forward in the direction of L2.	Orun ahp-gubi	Eolgul maggi
12	Kick with the left foot—ahp cha-gi—and place the foot on the ground in the direction of L2.	Owen ahp-gubi	Momtong bandae ji-ru-gi
13	Turn to the left on the ball of the right foot, and move the left foot in the direction B.	Orun ahp-gubi	Guduro-ahre maggi
14	Move right foot forward in the direction B.	Owen dwi-gubi	Guduro momtong maggi
15	Move left foot forward in the direction B.	Orun dwi-gubi	Momtong maggi
16	Move the right foot forward in the direction B.	Orun ahp-gubi	Momtong bandae ji-ru-gi (Kihop)
17	Turn to the left on the ball of the right foot, and move the left foot in the direction of L1.	Owen ahp-gubi	Eolgul maggi
18	Kick with the right foot—ahp cha-gi—and place the foot on the ground in the direction of L1.	Orun ahp-gubi	Momtong bandae ji-ru-gi
19	Turn 180 degrees to the right on the ball of the left foot, and move the right foot forward in the direction of R1.	Orun ahp-gubi	Eolgul maggi
20	Kick with the left foot—ahp cha-gi—and place the foot on the ground in the direction of R1.	Owen ahp-gubi	Momtong bandae ji-ru-gi
Guman	Turn to the left on the ball of the foot until you can look in the direction F.	Naranhi sogi	Gibon junbi

Pal-Gwe 3 Chang

	Body and Leg Movements	Stance	Hand Techniques
Junbi	Look in the direction F, and take one step to the side with the left foot.	Naranhi sogi	Gibon junbi
1	Turn to the left, and place the left foot one step in the direction of L1.	Owen ahp-gubi	Ahre maggi
2	Move the right foot forward one step in the direction of L1.	Orun ahp-gubi	Momtong bandae ji-ru-gi
3	Turn 180 degrees to the right on the ball of the left foot, and move the right foot forward in the direction of R1.	Orun ahp-gubi	Ahre maggi
4	Move the left foot one step forward in the direction of R1.	Owen ahp-gubi	Momtong bandae ji-ru-gi
5	Turn to the left on the ball of your right foot, and move the left foot forward in the direction of F.	Owen ahp-gubi	Ahre maggi
6	Move the right foot one step forward in the direction F.	Orun ahp-gubi	Eolgul maggi
7	Move the left foot one step forward in the direction F.	Owen ahp-gubi	Eolgul maggi
8	Move the right foot one step forward in the direction F.	Orun ahp-gubi	Eolgul bandae ji-ru-gi
9	Turn to your left on the ball of the right foot until you are able to place the left foot in the direction of R2.	Orun dwi-gubi	Son-nal momtong maggi
10	Move the right foot one step forward in the direction of R2.	Owen dwi-gubi	Son-nal momtong maggi

Continued on following pages.

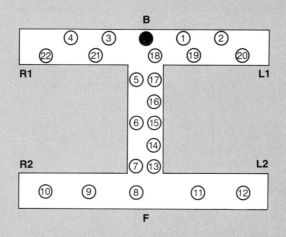

Pal-Gwe 3 Chang

	Body and Leg Movements	Stance	Hand Techniques
11	Turn 180 degrees to the right on the ball of the left foot, and move the right foot in the direction of L2.	Owen dwi-gubi	Son-nal momtong maggi
12	Move the left foot one step forward in the direction of L2.	Orun dwi-gubi	Son-nal momtong maggi
13	Turn left on the ball of your right foot, and move the left foot in the direction B.	Orun dwi-gubi	Momtong yop maggi ($\rightarrow$F)
14	Immediately change your position to face in the direction F.	Owen dwi-gubi	Momtong yop maggi ($\rightarrow$F)
15	Move right foot back in the direction B.	Orun dwi-gubi	Momtong maggi ($\rightarrow$F)
16	Move left foot back in the direction B.	Owen dwi-gubi	Momtong maggi ($\rightarrow$F)
17	Move right foot back in the direction B.	Orun dwi-gubi	Momtong maggi ($\rightarrow$F)
18	Immediately change your position in the direction B.	Owen dwi-gubi	Momtong maggi ($\rightarrow$F)
19	Turn 180 degrees to your left on the ball of the right foot, placing the left foot forward in the direction of L1.	Owen ahp-gubi	Eolgul maggi
20	Move your right foot forward in the direction of L1.	Orun ahp-gubi	Eolgul bandae ji-ru-gi
21	Turn 180 degrees to your right on the ball of your right foot, and move the foot forward in the direction of R1.	Orun ahp-gubi	Eolgul maggi
22	Move your left foot one step forward in the direction B.	Owen ahp-gubi	Eolgul bandae ji-ru-gi (Kihop)
Guman	Turn left on the ball of the right foot, and look in the direction F.	Naranhi sogi	Gibon junbi

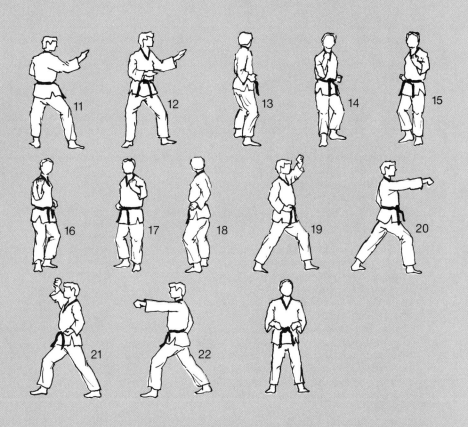

Pal-Gwe 4 Chang

	Body and Leg Movements	Stance	Hand Techniques
Junbi	Look in the direction F and move the left foot to the side.	Naranhi sogi	Gibon junbi
1	Turn to the left, and move the left foot forward in the direction of L1.	Orun dwi-gubi	Kum-kang momtong maggi
2	Stance remains unchanged.	Orun dwi-gubi	Dangyo-tok ji-ru-gi
3	Pull the left foot slightly towards the right foot.	Pyong-hi sogi	Owen han son-nal yop chi-gi
4	Assume a **modum-baal** stance by pulling the left leg towards the right leg, and then immediately move the left foot one step forward in the direction F.	Owen dwi-gubi	Kum-kang momtong maggi
5	Stance remains the same.	Owen dwi-gubi	Dangyo-tok ji-ru-gi
6	Pull the right foot slightly towards the left foot.	Pyong-hi sogi	Orun han son-nal yop chi-gi
7	Assume **modum-baal** stance by pulling the right foot towards the left foot, and immediately move the left foot one step forward in the direction F.	Orun dwi-gubi	Son-nal momtong maggi
8	With the left foot kick—**ahp cha-gi**—and then place the foot in the direction F.	Orun ahp-gubi	Pyong sonkut sewo chi-ru-gi
9	Turn—in place—to the left, and carry out a **miduro paegi** with the right hand; immediately turn around 360 degrees on the ball of the right foot; place the left foot one step forward in the direction F.	Owen ahp-gubi	Owen me-joomok bakkat chi-gi
10	Move the right foot forward in the direction F.	Orun ahp-gubi	Momtong bandae ji-ru-gi (Kihop)
11	Turn to the left on the ball of the right foot, and place the foot forward in the direction of R2.	Orun dwi-gubi	Kum-kang momtong maggi

Continued on following pages.

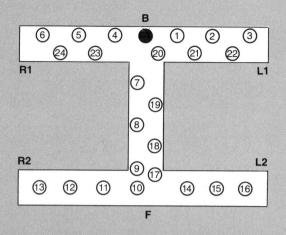

Pal-Gwe 4 Chang

	Body and Leg Movements	Stance	Hand Techniques
12	Stance remains unchanged.	Orun dwi-gubi	Dangyo tok ji-ru-gi
13	Pull left foot slightly towards the right foot.	Pyong-hi sogi	Orun han son-nal yop chi-gi
14	Assume **modum-baal** by pulling the right foot towards the left and immediately point the right foot forward in the direction of **L2**.	Owen dwi-gubi	Kum-kang momtong maggi
15	Stance remains unchanged.	Owen dwi-gubi	Dangyo tok ji-ru-gi
16	Pull the right foot slightly towards the left.	Pyong-hi sogi	Owen han son-nal yop chi-gi
17	Assume **modum-baal** by pulling the right foot towards the left, and abruptly move the left foot in the direction **B**.	Orun dwi-gubi	Son-nal momtong maggi
18	Kick with the right foot—**ahp cha-gi**—and place the foot back on the ground in the direction **B**.	Orun ahp-gubi	Pyong sonkut sewo chi-ru-gi
19	Immediately turn to your left and carry out a **wiro paegi**; then quickly turn 360 degrees on your right foot, and move the left foot one step forward in the direction **B**.	Owen ahp-gubi	Owen me-joomok bakkat chi-gi
20	Move right foot one step forward in the direction **B**.	Orun ahp-gubi	Momtong bandae ji-ru-gi (Kihop)
21	Turn to the left on the ball of your right foot, and move the left foot forward in the direction of **L1**.	Juchoom sogi	Ahrē yop maggi
22	Push the left foot forward in the direction of **L1**.	Owen ahp-gubi	Momtong baro ji-ru-gi
23	Pull the left foot slightly towards yourself, and turn your body in the direction **F**; eyes look in the direction of **R1**.	Juchoom sogi	Ahre yop maggi
24	Push the right foot forward slightly in the direction of **R1**.	Orun ahp-gubi	Momtong baro ji-ru-gi
Guman	Pull the right foot slightly towards yourself and look in the direction **V**.	Naranhi sogi	Gibon junbi

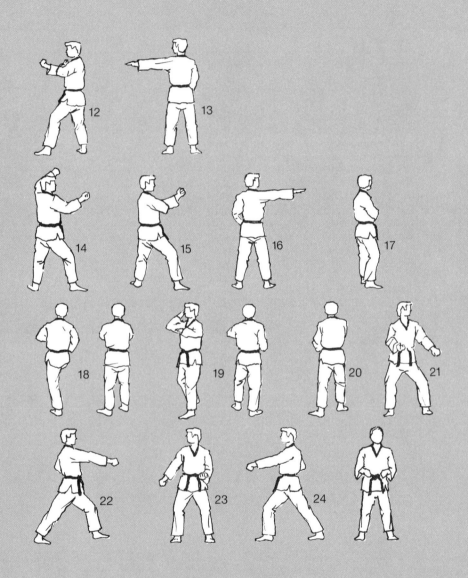

Pal-Gwe 5 Chang

	Body and Leg Movements	Stance	Hand Techniques
Junbi	Look in the direction F, and move left leg sideways.	Naranhi sogi	Gibon junbi
1	Move the left foot back one step in the direction B.	Orun ahp-gubi	Gawi maggi
2	Move the left foot forward one step; then move the right foot in the direction of L1 without moving the left foot.	Orun dwi-gubi	Son-nal ahre maggi
3	Move the right foot one step forward in the direction of L1.	Owen dwi-gubi	Son-nal momtong maggi
4	Move the right leg one step backwards in the direction of R1.	Orun dwi-gubi	Owen batangson nullo maggi
5	Move the right leg again one step forward in the direction of L1.	Orun ahp-gubi	Momtong bandae ji-ru-gi
6	Turn 180 degrees to the right on the ball of the left foot, and place the right foot in the direction of R1.	Owen dwi-gubi	Son-nal ahre maggi
7	Move the left foot one step forward in the direction of R1.	Orun dwi-gubi	Son-nal momtong maggi
8	Move the left foot back one step in the direction of R1.	Owen dwi-gubi	Orun batangson nullo maggi
9	Move the left foot one step forward in the direction of R1.	Owen ahp-gubi	Momtong bandae ji-ru-gi

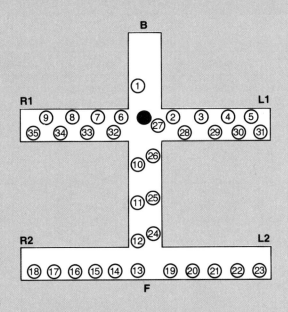

Pal-Gwe 5 Chang

	Body and Leg Movements	Stance	Hand Techniques
10	Turn to your left on the ball of the right foot, and place the left foot in the direction F.	Owen ahp-gubi	Gawi maggi
11	Move the right foot forward in the direction F.	Orun ahp-gubi	Guduro-momtong maggi
12	Move the left foot forward in the direction F.	Owen ahp-gubi	Guduro-momtong maggi
13	Move the right foot forward in the direction F.	Orun ahp-gubi	Pyong sonkut sewo ji-ru-gi (Kihop)
14	Turn left on the ball of the right foot, and place the left foot in the direction of R2.	Owen ahp-gubi	Owen an palmok momtong bakkat maggi
15	Stance remains unchanged.	Owen ahp-gubi	Momtong dubon ji-ru-gi
16	Lift the left foot to knee-height while still looking in the direction of R2.	Orun hakdari sogi	Orun jagun dolchogwi
17	Kick with the left foot—yop cha-gi—placing the foot down in the direction of R2.	Owen ahp-gubi	Orun palkoop
18	Move the right foot forward in the direction of R2.	Owen dwi-gubi	Son-nal momtong maggi
19	Turn to the right 180 degrees on the ball of the left foot, and move the right foot forward in the direction of L2.	Orun ahp-gubi	Orun an palmok momtong bakkat maggi
20	Stance remains unchanged.	Orun ahp-gubi	Momtong dubon ji-ru-gi (left to right)
21	Lift right foot to knee-height while continuing to look in the direction of L2.	Owen hakdari sogi	Orun jagun dolchogwi
22	Kick with the right leg—yop cha-gi—and set the foot down in the direction of L2.	Orun ahp-gubi	Owen palkoop pyojok chi-gi
23	Move the left foot forward in the direction of L2.	Orun dwi-gubi	Son-nal momtong maggi

Continued on following pages.

	Body and Leg Movements	Stance	Hand Techniques
24	Turn to your left on the ball of the right foot and move the left foot forward in the direction B.	Owen ahp-gubi	Gawi maggi
25	Move the right foot forward in the direction B.	Owen dwi-gubi	Guduro ahre maggi
26	Move the left foot forward in the direction B.	Orun dwi maggi	Guduro ahre maggi
27	Move the right foot forward in the direction B.	Owen ahp maggi	Momtong bandae ji-ru-gi (Kihop)
28	Turn to the left on the ball of the right foot, and move the left foot forward in the direction of L1.	Orun dwi-gubi	Son-nal ahre maggi
29	Move the right foot forward in the direction of L1.	Owen dwi-gubi	Son-nal momtong maggi
30	Move the right foot back one step in the direction of R1, but continue to look in the direction of L1.	Orun dwi-gubi	Owen batangson nullo maggi
31	Move the right foot again one step forward in the direction of L1.	Orun ahp-gubi	Momtong bandae ji-ru-gi
32	Turn 180 degrees to the right on the left foot, and move the right foot in the direction of R1.	Owen dwi-gubi	Son-nal ahre maggi
33	Move the left foot forward in the direction of R1.	Orun dwi-gubi	Son-nal momtong maggi
34	Move the left foot again one step back in the direction of L1; continue looking in the direction of R1.	Owen dwi-gubi	Momtong bandae ji-ru-gi
Guman	Turn left on the ball of the right foot in the direction F and, at the same time, pull the left foot to the right.	Naranhi sogi	Gibon junbi

Pal-Gwe 6 Chang

	Body and Leg Movements	Stance	Hand Techniques
Junbi	Look in the direction F, and move the left foot to the side.	Naranhi sogi	Gibon junbi
1	Turn to the left, and move the left foot in the direction of L1.	Orun dwi-gubi	Son-nal momtong maggi
2	Kick—ahp cha-gi—and then set the foot down pointing in the direction of L1.	Orun ahp-gubi	Momtong bandae ji-ru-gi
3	Turn 180 degrees to the right on the ball of the left right, then move the right foot forward in the direction of R1.	Owen dwi-gubi	Son-nal momtong maggi
4	Kick with the left leg—ahp cha-gi—setting the foot down in the direction of R1.	Owen dwi-gubi	Momtong bandae ji-ru-gi
5	Turn to the left on the ball of the right foot, and move the left foot forward in the direction F.	Owen ahp-gubi	Ahre maggi
6	Turn to the left without changing your stance.	Owen ahp-gubi	Jebipum mok chi-gi
7	Kick—ahp cha-gi—and jump forward one step in the direction F.	Orun koa sogi	Guduro dung-joomok eolgul ahp chi-gi (Kihop)
8	Turn to the left on the ball of the right foot, and move the left foot in the direction of R2.	Orun dwi-gubi	Son-nal ahre maggi
9	Push the left foot slightly in the direction of R2, leaving the right foot in place.	Owen ahp-gubi	Momtong hecho maggi

Continued on following pages.

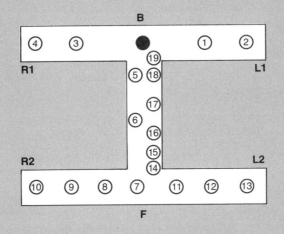

Pal-Gwe 6 Chang

	Body and Leg Movements	Stance	Hand Techniques
10	Kick with the right leg—ahp cha-gi—and place the foot afterward in the direction of R2.	Orun ahp-gubi	Momtong dubon ji-ru-gi (right to left)
11	Turn 180 degrees to the right on the ball of the left foot, and move the right foot forward in the direction of L2.	Owen dwi-gubi	Son-nal ahre maggi
12	Push the right foot forward in the direction of L2; the left foot remains in place.	Orun ahp-gubi	Momtong hecho maggi
13	Kick with the left leg—ahp cha-gi—and place the foot on the ground in the direction of L2.	Owen ahp-gubi	Momtong dubon ji-ru-gi (left to right)
14	Turn to the left on the ball of the right foot, and move the left foot in the direction B.	Orun dwi-gubi	Son-nal momtong maggi
15	Push the left foot slightly in the direction B, and turn the upper body slightly to the left without moving the right foot.	Owen ahp-gubi	Jebipum tok chi-gi
16	Kick with the right leg—ahp cha-gi—and set the foot on the ground in the direction B.	Orun ahp-gubi	Orun dung-joomok eolgul ahp chi-gi (Kihop)
17	Kick with the left leg—ahp cha-gi—and set the right foot on the ground in the direction B.	Owen ahp-gubi	Eolgul maggi
18	Kick with the right leg—yop cha-gi—in the direction B, setting the foot down pointing in the same direction.	Owen dwi-gubi	Son-nal momtong maggi
19	Immediately change your position by turning in the direction F.	Orun dwi-gubi	Son-nal momtong maggi
Guman	Pull the right foot slightly towards the left foot.	Naranhi sogi	Gibon junbi

Pal-Gwe 7 Chang

	Body and Leg Movements	Stance	Hand Techniques
Junbi	Look in the direction F, and move the left foot to the side.	Naranhi sogi	Gibon junbi
1	Move the left foot forward in the direction F.	Owen ahp-gubi	Hecho ahre maggi
2	Kick with the left leg—ahp cha-gi—and set the foot on the ground in the direction F.	Orun ahp-gubi	An palmok hecho momtong maggi
3	Kick with the right leg—ahp cha-gi—and set the foot down in the direction F.	Orun ahp-gubi	Otgoro eolgul maggi
4	Kick with the right leg—yop cha-gi—in the direction F, setting the foot down pointing in the same direction.	Owen dwi-gubi	Son-nal momtong maggi
5	Turn to the left on the ball of your right foot, and place the left foot in the direction R.	Orun dwi-gubi	Momtong yop maggi
6	Push the left foot slightly forward in the direction R.	Owen ahp-gubi	Eolgul baro ji-ru-gi
7	Stance remains unchanged.	Owen ahp-gubi	Eolgul maggi
8	Kick with the right foot—yop cha-gi—placing the foot down in the direction R.	Orun dwi-gubi	Son-nal ahre maggi
9	Push the right foot forward in the direction R.	Orun ahp-gubi	Momtong baro ji-ru-gi
10	Turn 180 degrees to the right on the ball of the left foot, moving the right foot in the direction L.	Owen dwi-gubi	Momtong yop maggi
11	Push the right foot forward slightly in the direction L.	Orun ahp-gubi	Eolgul baro ji-ru-gi
12	Stance remains unchanged.	Orun ahp-gubi	Eolgul maggi

Continued on following pages.

Pal-Gwe 7 Chang

	Body and Leg Movements	Stance	Hand Techniques
13	Kick with the left leg—yop cha-gi—and place the foot in the direction L.	Orun dwi-gubi	Son-nal ahre maggi
14	Push the left foot forward slightly in the direction L.	Owen ahp-gubi	Momtong baro ji-ru-gi
15	Turn to the left on the ball of the right foot, placing the left foot in the direction B.	Owen ahp-gubi	Otgoro-ahre maggi
16	Stance remains unchanged.	Owen ahp-gubi	Otgoro-eolgul maggi
17	Open left fist; while pulling the right fist back to the hips, reach with the left for defense; right fist carries out a punch while the left hand is pulling back to the hip.	Owen ahp-gubi	Eolgul baro ji-ru-gi (Kihop)
18	Turn your body to the left on the ball of your left foot and, at the end of the turn, place your right foot—having completed a full circle—forcefully to the ground in the direction F while looking in the direction F.	Juchoom sogi	Ahre yop maggi (→F)
19	Turn to your left without changing the position of the right foot, pushing the left foot slightly in the direction B.	Owen ahp-gubi	Owen han son-nal eolgul bakkat chi-gi
20	Turn left on the ball of your left foot and carry out a pyojok cha-gi in the direction R; place the right foot in the direction B.	Juchoom sogi (→R)	Orun palkoop pyojok chi-gi (→R)
21	Carry out a mikurum-baal in the direction B.	Juchoom sogi	Owen-santul maggi
22	Carry out a mikurum-baal in the direction B.	Orun dwi-gubi	Son-nal momtong maggi (→V)
23	Push the left foot slightly in the direction F.	Owen ahp-gubi	Momtong baro ji-ru-gi (Kihop)
Guman	Pull the left foot towards the right while looking in the direction F.	Naranhi sogi	Gibon junbi

Pal-Gwe 8 Chang

	Body and Leg Movements	Stance	Hand Techniques
Junbi	Look in the direction F, and move the left foot to the outside.	Naranhi sogi	Gibon junbi
1	Turn to the left, and move the left foot forward in the direction of L1.	Owen ahp-gubi	Ahre maggi
2	Turn your body back to the right and pull the left foot slightly towards the right foot; at the same time turn full circle with the left arm straight to the outside, directly in front of the body at shoulder-height.	Owen sogi	Me-joomok naeryo chi-gi (→L1)
3	Move the right foot forward one step in the direction of L1.	Orun ahp-gubi	Momtong bandae chi-ru-gi
4	Turn 180 degrees to the right on the ball of the left foot, and place the right foot in the direction of R1.	Orun ahp-gubi	Ahre maggi
5	Turn the body back slightly to the left, and pull the right foot slightly towards the left foot; at the same time turn full circle with the right arm outstretched to the outside at shoulder-height, directly in front of your body.	Orun sogi	Me-joomok naeryo chi-gi (→R1)
6	Move the right foot forward in the direction of R1.	Owen ahp-gubi	Momtong bandae ji-ru-gi
7	Turn to the left on the ball of the right foot, and place the left foot in the direction F.	Orun ahp-gubi	Son-nal momtong maggi
8	Move the right foot forward in the direction F.	Orun ahp-gubi	Pyong sonkut sewo chi-ru-gi

Continued on following pages.

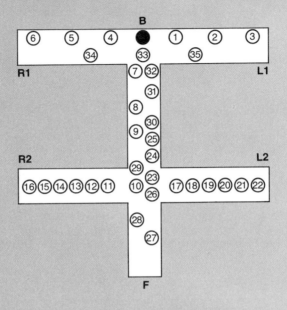

	Body and Leg Movements	Stance	Hand Techniques
9	Turn your body to the left, moving your center of gravity forward; then turn on the right foot 360 degrees to your left until you are able to set the foot on the ground in the direction F.	Orun dwi-gubi	Owen dung-joomok bakkat chi-gi
10	Move the right foot one step forward in the direction F.	Orun ahp-gubi	Eolgul bandae ji-ru-gi (Kihop)
11	Turn to the left on the ball of the right foot, placing the left foot in the direction of R2.	Orun dwi-gubi	Owen han son-nal yop sogi
12	Turn slightly to the right and quickly move the left foot slightly in the direction B, but continue looking in the direction of R2.	Owen mojuchoom sogi	Sonmok paegi
13	Quickly turn to the left, placing the left foot again in the direction of R2.	Juchoom sogi	Palkoop yop chi-gi (→R2)
14	Turn the body a bit more to the right, pushing the left foot forward in the direction of R2.	Owen ahp-gubi	Momtong bakkat maggi
15	Stance remains unchanged.	Owen ahp-gubi	Momtong baro ji-ru-gi
16	Turn 180 degrees on the right foot in the direction B.	Juchoom sogi	Owen jagun dolchogwi
17	Carry out a **modum-baal** by pulling the left foot towards the right and immediately moving the right foot in the direction of L2.	Owen dwi-gubi	Orun han son-nal yop chi-gi
18	Quickly turn body slightly to the left, and place the right foot slightly in the direction B while continuing to look in the direction of L2.	Orun mojuchoom sogi	Sonmok paegi
19	Turn to the right, and quickly push the right foot forward again in the direction of L2.	Juchoom sogi	Palkoop yop chi-gi

Continued on following pages.

Pal-Gwe 8 Chang

	Body and Leg Movements	Stance	Hand Techniques
20	Turn further to the right, and push the right foot in the direction of L2.	Orun ahp-gubi	Momtong bakkat maggi
21	Stance remains unchanged.	Orun ahp-gubi	Momtong baro ji-ru-gi
22	Turn to the left on the left foot as you pull the right foot somewhat towards the left.	Juchoom sogi	Orun jagun dolchogwi (→B)
23	Carry out a **modum-baal** by pulling the right foot towards the left; quickly pull the left foot up to knee-height while turning to the right.	Orun hakdari sogi	Orun jagun dolchogwi (looking towards B; body towards L)
24	Kick with your left leg—yop cha-gi—in the direction B, placing the foot down in the same direction.	Owen ahp-gubi	Palkoop pyojok chi-gi
25	Turn to the right on the right leg, pulling the left foot slightly to the right.	Juchoom sogi	Owen jagun dolchogwi (looking towards F; body towards L)
26	Carry out a **modum-baal** by pulling the left foot towards the right and immediately pulling the right leg up to knee-height.	Owen hakdari sogi	Owen jagun dolchogwi
27	Kick with the right leg—yop cha-gi—in the direction F, placing the foot on the ground in the same direction.	Orun ahp-gubi	Palkoop pyojok chi-gi
28	Turn to the left on the right foot in the direction B.	Owen ahp-gubi	Momtong hecho maggi
	Pull both fists (back of fists pointing up) to the hips without moving the legs.	Owen ahp-gubi	Du-joomok jechyo ji-ru-gi
29	Place the right foot one step forward in the direction B.	Orun ahp-gubi	Momtong hecho maggi
	Then pull fists back towards the hips without moving the legs.	Orun ahp-gubi	Du-joomok jechyo ji-ru-gi

Continued on following pages.

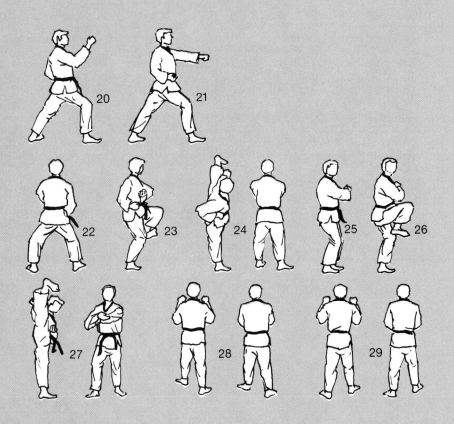

Pal-Gwe 8 Chang

	Body and Leg Movements	Stance	Hand Techniques
30	Move left foot forward in the direction B.	Orun dwi-gubi	Han son-nal momtong maggi
31	Turn the left hand (grabbing motion), pulling it back to the left hip while turning to the right and placing the right foot in the direction H.	Juchoom sogi	Orun palkoop dwi chi-gi (looking L; body towards R)
32	Turn to the left on the right foot in the direction F, and carry out a **modum-baal** with the left foot.	Moa sogi (very slowly)	Gyop-son
33	Abruptly move the left foot in the direction of L1 while lowering the body.	Juchoom sogi	Monge paegi
34	Change position by carrying out a **mikurum-baal** in the direction of R1.	Juchoom sogi	Owen dwi ji-ru-gi (Kihop)
Guman	Pull the left foot to the right and look in the direction F.	Naranhi sogi	Gibon junbi

Tae-Kook 1 Chang

	Body and Leg Movements	Stance	Hand Techniques
Junbi	Look in the direction F, and set left foot to the side.	Naranhi sogi	Gibon junbi
1	Turn to your left, and place the left foot in the direction of L1.	Owen ahp sogi	Ahre maggi
2	Move the right foot one step forward in the direction of L1.	Orun ahp sogi	Momtong bandae ji-ru-gi
3	Turn 180 degrees to the right on the ball of the left foot until the right foot can be placed in the direction of R1.	Orun ahp sogi	Ahre maggi
4	Move the left foot one step forward in the direction of R1.	Owen ahp sogi	Momtong bandae ji-ru-gi
5	Turn to the left on the ball of the right foot, and move the left foot one step in the direction F.	Owen ahp-gubi	Ahre maggi
6	Body position and stance remain unchanged.	Owen ahp-gubi	Momtong baro ji-ru-gi
7	Move the right foot one step in the direction of R2 while keeping the left foot in place.	Owen ahp sogi	Momtong an maggi
8	Move the left foot one step forward in the direction of R2.	Owen ahp sogi	Momtong baro ji-ru-gi
9	Turn left 180 degrees on the ball of the right foot until the left foot can be placed in the direction of L2.	Owen ahp sogi	Momtong an maggi
10	Move the right foot one step forward in the direction of L2.	Orun ahp sogi	Momtong baro maggi

Continued on following pages.

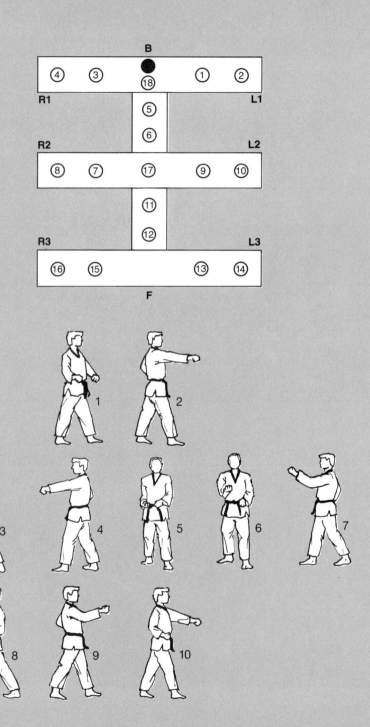

Tae-Kook 1 Chang

	Body and Leg Movements	Stance	Hand Techniques
11	Turn to the right on the ball of the left foot, and move the right foot one step forward in the direction F.	Orun ahp-gubi	Ahre maggi
12	Body position and stance remain unchanged.	Orun ahp-gubi	Momtong baro ji-ru-gi
13	Turn left on the right foot, and place the left foot in the direction of L3.	Owen ahp sogi	Eolgul maggi
14	Kick with the right leg—ahp cha-gi—placing the foot in the direction of L3.	Orun ahp sogi	Momtong bandae ji-ru-gi
15	Turn 180 degrees right on the left foot, and move one step in the direction of R3.	Orun ahp sogi	Eolgul maggi
16	Kick with the left leg—ahp cha-gi—placing the foot in the direction of R3.	Owen ahp sogi	Momtong bandae ji-ru-gi
17	Using the right foot as a pivot, turn the body to the right and place the left foot one step in the direction B.	Owen ahp-gubi	Ahre maggi
18	Move the right foot one step forward in the direction B.	Orun ahp-gubi	Momtong bandae ji-ru-gi (Kihop)
Guman	Make a full turn to the left on the ball of your right foot until you can look in the direction F.	Naranhi sogi	Gibon junbi

Tae-Kook 2 Chang

	Body and Leg Movements	Stance	Hand Techniques
Junbi	Look in the direction F, and move the left foot to the side.	Naranhi sogi	Gibon junbi
1	Turn to the left, and move the left foot forward in the direction of L1.	Owen ahp sogi	Ahre maggi
2	Move the right foot one step forward in the direction of L1.	Orun ahp-gubi	Momtong bandae ji-ru-gi
3	Turn right on the ball of the left foot until you are able to place the right foot in the direction of R1.	Orun ahp sogi	Ahre maggi
4	Move the left foot one step forward in the direction of R1.	Owen ahp-gubi	Momtong bandae ji-ru-gi
5	Turn left on the ball of the right foot, and move one step in the direction F.	Owen ahp sogi	Momtong an maggi
6	Move the right foot in the direction F.	Orun ahp sogi	Momtong an maggi
7	Turn to the left on the ball of the right foot, and place the left foot one step in the direction of L2.	Owen ahp sogi	Ahre maggi
8	Kick with the right leg—ahp cha-gi—and set the foot in the direction of L2.	Orun ahp-gubi	Eolgul bandae ji-ru-gi
9	Turn right on the ball of the left foot until you can place the right foot in the direction of R2.	Orun ahp sogi	Ahre maggi

Continued on following pages.

Tae-Kook 2 Chang

	Body and Leg Movements	Stance	Hand Techniques
10	Kick with the left foot—ahp cha-gi hecho—and place the foot in the direction of R2.	Owen ahp-gubi	Eolgul bandae ji-ru-gi
11	Turn to the left on the ball of the right foot, and place the left foot one step in the direction F.	Owen ahp sogi	Eolgul maggi
12	Move the right foot one step in the direction F.	Orun ahp sogi	Eolgul maggi
13	Turn to the left on the ball of the right foot, and place the left foot one step forward in the direction of R3.	Owen ahp sogi	Momtong an maggi
14	Turn 180 degrees to the right on the ball of the left foot, and place the right foot in the direction of L3.	Orun ahp sogi	Momtong an maggi
15	Turn to the left, and place the left foot in the direction B without moving the right foot.	Owen ahp sogi	Ahre maggi
16	Kick with the right leg—ahp cha-gi— placing the foot in the direction B.	Orun ahp sogi	Momtong bandae ji-ru-gi
17	Kick with the left leg—ahp cha-gi— placing the foot in the direction B.	Owen ahp sogi	Momtong bandae ji-ru-gi
18	Again, kick with the right foot—ahp cha-gi—and place the foot in the direction B.	Orun ahp sogi	Momtong bandae ji-ru-gi (Kihop)
Guman	Turn left on the ball of the right foot until you can look in the direction F.	Naranhi sogi	Gibon junbi

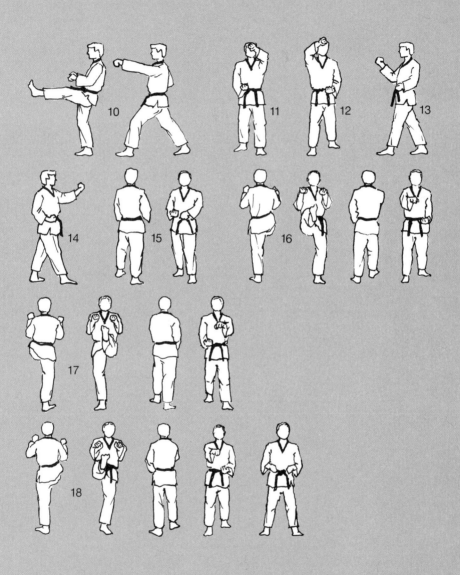

Tae-Kook 3 Chang

	Body and Leg Movements	Stance	Hand Techniques
Junbi	Look in the direction F, and move the left foot sideways.	Naranhi sogi	Gibon junbi
1	Turn to your left, and move the left foot one step forward in the direction of L1.	Owen ahp sogi	Ahre maggi
2	Kick with the right leg—ahp cha-gi—placing the foot in the direction of L1.	Orun ahp-gubi	Momtong dubon ji-ru-gi (right to left)
3	Turn 180 degrees to the right with the left leg; set the foot in the direction of R1.	Orun ahp sogi	Ahre maggi
4	Kick with the left leg—ahp cha-gi—and place the foot in the direction of R1.	Owen ahp-gubi	Momtong dubon ji-ru-gi (left to right)
5	Turn to the left on the ball of the right foot, moving the left foot one step forward in the direction F.	Owen ahp sogi	Orun son-nal an chi-gi (orun son-nal mok chi-gi)
6	Move the right foot forward in the direction F.	Orun ahp sogi	Owen son-nal an chi-gi (owen son-nal mok chi-gi)
7	Move the left foot forward one step in the direction of L2 without moving the right leg.	Orun dwi-gubi	Owen han son-nal momtong yop maggi
8	Without moving the right foot, place the left foot slightly in the direction of L2.	Owen ahp-gubi	Momtong baro ji-ru-gi
9	Standing on the left foot, turn the body 180 degrees in the direction of R2.	Owen dwi-gubi	Orun han son-nal momtong yop maggi
10	Slightly move the right foot in the direction of R2.	Orun ahp-gubi	Momtong baro ji-ru-gi

Continued on following pages.

Tae-Kook 3 Chang

	Body and Leg Movements	Stance	Hand Techniques
11	Without moving the right foot, place the left foot in the direction F.	Owen ahp sogi	Momtong an maggi
12	Move the right foot forward in the direction F.	Orun ahp sogi	Momtong an maggi
13	Turn your body to the left on the ball of the right foot, placing the left foot in the direction of R3.	Owen ahp sogi	Ahre maggi
14	Kick with the right leg—ahp cha-gi—setting the foot down in the direction of R3.	Orun ahp-gubi	Momtong dubon ji-ru-gi (right to left)
15	On your left foot turn your body 180 degrees to the right, moving the right foot forward in the direction of L3.	Orun ahp sogi	Ahre maggi
16	Kick with the left leg—ahp cha-gi—placing the foot in the direction of L3.	Owen ahp-gubi	Momtong dubon ji-ru-gi (left to right)
17	Turn to the left on the ball of the right foot, placing the left foot in the direction B.	Owen ahp sogi	Ahre maggi (then quickly) momtong baro ji-ru-gi
18	Move the right foot forward one step in the direction B.	Orun ahp sogi	Ahre maggi (then quickly) momtong baro ji-ru-gi
19	Kick with the left leg—ahp cha-gi—placing the foot in the direction B.	Owen ahp sogi	Ahre maggi (then quickly) momtong baro ji-ru-gi
20	Kick with the right leg—ahp cha-gi—placing the foot in the direction B.	Orun ahp sogi	Ahre maggi (then quickly) momtong baro ji-ru-gi
Guman	Turn your body on the ball of the right foot to the left until you can look in the direction F.	Naranhi sogi	Gibon junbi

Tae-Kook 4 Chang

	Body and Leg Movements	Stance	Hand Techniques
Junbi	Look in the direction F, and move the left foot to the side.	Naranhi sogi	Gibon junbi
1	Turn the body to the left, and move the left foot one step forward in the direction of **L1**.	Orun dwi-gubi	Son-nal momtong maggi
2	Move the right foot forward one step in the direction of **L1**.	Orun ahp-gubi	Orun sonkut sewo ji-ru-gi
3	Turn 180 degrees to the right on the ball of the left foot, moving the right foot forward one step in the direction of **R1**.	Owen dwi-gubi	Son-nal momtong maggi
4	Move the left foot one step forward in the direction of **R1**.	Owen ahp-gubi	Owen sonkut sewo ji-ru-gi
5	Turn to the left on the ball of the right foot, moving the left foot one step forward in the direction F.	Owen ahp-gubi	Jebipum mok chi-gi
6	Kick with the right leg—ahp cha-gi—placing the foot in the direction F.	Orun ahp-gubi	Momtong baro ji-ru-gi
7	Kick with the left leg—yop cha-gi—without changing the stance of the right foot, placing the left foot in the direction F.		(Carry this movement out as quickly as possible.)
8	Kick with the right leg—yop cha-gi—without having changed the stance, and set the right foot down in the direction F.	Owen dwi-gubi	Son-nal momtong maggi
9	Turn to the left on the ball of the left foot until the left foot can move forward in the direction of **R3**.	Orun dwi-gubi	Momtong bakkat maggi

Continued on following pages.

Tae-Kook 4 Chang

	Body and Leg Movements	Stance	Hand Techniques
10	While the left foot remains in place, kick with the right foot—**ahp cha-gi**—then return the right foot to the previous position.	Orun dwi-gubi	Momtong an maggi
11	Turn the body 180 degrees to the right in the direction of L3.	Owen dwi-gubi	Momtong hakkat maggi
12	While the right foot remains in place, kick with the left leg—**ahp cha-gi**—setting the foot down in the previous place.	Owen dwi-gubi	Momtong an maggi
13	Move the left foot forward one step in the direction B while the right foot remains in place.	Owen ahp-gubi	Jebipum mok chi-gi
14	Kick with the right leg—**ahp cha-gi**—and then move the foot one step in the direction B.	Orun ahp-gubi	Orun dung-joomok eolgul ahp chi-gi
15	Move the left foot to the right in the direction of R2 without changing the orientation of the right foot.	Owen ahp sogi	Momtong maggi
16	Stance remains unchanged.	Owen ahp sogi	Momtong baro ji-ru-gi
17	Turn the body 180 degrees to the right—in place—until you can look in the direction of L2.	Orun ahp sogi	Momtong maggi
18	Stance remains unchanged.	Orun ahp sogi	Momtong baro ji-ru-gi
19	Move the left foot forward in the direction B while the right foot remains in place.	Owen ahp-gubi	Momtong maggi (then quickly) momtong dubon ji-ru-gi (right to left)
20	Move the right foot forward in the direction B.	Orun ahp-gubi	Momtong maggi (then quickly) momtong dubon ji-ru-gi (left to right) (Kihop)
Guman	Turn left on the ball of the right foot until you are able to look in the direction F.	Naranhi sogi	Gibon junbi

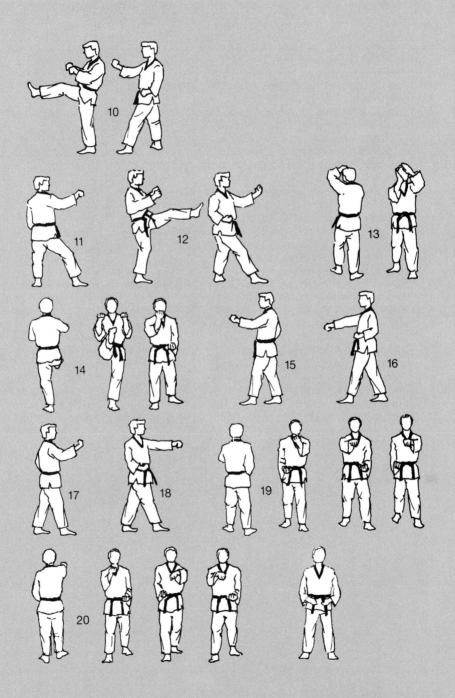

	Body and Leg Movements	Stance	Hand Techniques
Junbi	Look in the direction F while moving the left foot sideways.	Naranhi sogi	Gibon junbi
1	Turn your body to the left, and move the left foot forward in the direction of **L1**.	Owen ahp-gubi	Ahre maggi
2	Straighten your body while pulling the left foot towards the right; at the same time quickly move the left fist close to the body in an upward circle.	Owen sogi	Me-joomok naeryo chi-gi
3	Turn 180 degrees to the right on the ball of the left foot, and move the foot one step forward in the direction of **R1**.	Orun ahp-gubi	Ahre maggi
4	Straighten the body while the right foot is pulled towards the left; at the same time quickly move the right fist close to the body in an upward circle.	Orun sogi	Me-joomok naeryo chi-gi
5	Move the left foot one step forward in the direction F without moving the right foot.	Owen ahp-gubi	Momtong maggi (then) momtong an maggi
6	Kick with the right foot—ahp cha-gi—placing the foot forward on the ground in the direction F.	Orun ahp-gubi	Orun dung-joomok eolgul ahp chi-gi (then) momtong an maggi
7	Kick with the left leg—ahp cha-gi—setting the foot down in the direction F.	Owen ahp-gubi	Owen dung-joomok eolgul ahp chi-gi (then) momtong an maggi
8	Move the right foot one step forward in the direction F.	Orun ahp-gubi	Orun dung-joomok eolgul ahp chi-gi
9	Turn to the left on the ball of the right foot, moving the foot one step forward in the direction of **R3**.	Orun dwi-gubi	Owen han son-nal momtong yop maggi
10	Move the right foot one step forward in the direction of **R3**.	Orun ahp-gubi	Orun palkoop momtong chi-gi

Continued on following pages.

Tae-Kook 5 Chang

	Body and Leg Movements	Stance	Hand Techniques
11	Turn 180 degrees to the right on the ball of the left foot, placing the right foot forward in the direction of L3.	Owen dwi-gubi	Orun han son-nal momtong yop maggi
12	Move the left foot forward one step in the direction of L3.	Owen ahp-gubi	Owen palkoop momtong chi-gi
13	Turn to the left on the ball of the right foot, moving the left foot one step forward in the direction B.	Owen ahp-gubi	Ahre maggi (then) momtong an maggi
14	Kick with the right leg—ahp cha-gi— placing the foot down in the direction B.	Orun ahp-gubi	Ahre maggi (then) momtong an maggi
15	Move the left foot in the direction of R2 without changing the right foot.	Owen ahp-gubi	Eolgul maggi
16	Kick with the right leg—yop cha-gi— placing the foot in the direction of R2.	Orun ahp-gubi	Owen palkoop momtong pyojok chi-gi
17	Turn 180 degrees to the right on the ball of the left foot, placing the right foot on the ground in the direction of L2.	Orun ahp-gubi	Eolgul maggi
18	Kick with the left leg—yop cha-gi— placing the foot on the ground in the direction of L2.	Owen ahp-gubi	Orun palkoop momtong pyojok chi-gi
19	Turn left on the ball of the right foot, moving the left foot forward in the direction B.	Owen ahp-gubi	Ahre maggi (then quickly) momtong an maggi
20	Kick with the right leg—ahp cha-gi— placing the foot on the ground in a jumping movement one step forward in the direction B.	Dwi koa sogi	Orun dung-joomok eolgul ahp chi-gi (swiftly) (Kihop)
Guman	Turn on the ball of the right foot to your left until you are able to look in the direction F.	Naranhi sogi	Gibon junbi

Tae-Kook 6 Chang

	Body and Leg Movements	Stance	Hand Techniques
Junbi	Move the left foot one step to the side, and look in the direction F.	Naranhi sogi	Gibon junbi
1	Turn to your left, and place the left foot in the direction F.	Owen ahp-gubi	Ahre maggi
2	Kick with the right leg—ahp cha-gi—returning the foot to its original position; the left foot is moved back slightly for the dwi-gubi.	Orun dwi-gubi	Momtong bakkat maggi
3	Turn 180 degrees to the right on the left leg in the direction of R1.	Orun ahp-gubi	Ahre maggi
4	Kick with the left leg—ahp cha-gi—returning the left foot to its original position; the right foot is moved back slightly for the dwi-gubi.	Owen dwi-gubi	Momtong bakkat maggi
5	Turn to the left on the right foot, placing the left foot in the direction F.	Owen ahp-gubi	Han son-nal bituro maggi
6	Kick a dolryo cha-gi with the right leg, placing the foot in the direction F.		
	Quickly move the left foot one step forward in the direction of L2.	Owen ahp-gubi	Eolgul bakkat maggi (then) momtong baro ji-ru-gi
7	Kick with the right leg—ahp cha-gi—placing the right foot in the direction of L2.	Orun ahp-gubi	Momtong baro ji-ru-gi
8	Turn 180 degrees to the right on the ball of the left foot, moving the right foot forward in the direction of R2.	Orun ahp-gubi	Eolgul bakkat maggi (then) momtong baro ji-ru-gi
9	Kick with the left leg—ahp cha-gi—placing the foot in the direction of R2.	Owen ahp-gubi	Momtong baro ji-ru-gi

Continued on following pages.

	Body and Leg Movements	Stance	Hand Techniques
10	Turn to the left on the ball of the right foot, and look in the direction F.	Naranhi sogi	Ahre hecho maggi
11	Move the right foot forward in the direction F.	Orun ahp-gubi	Han son-nal bituro maggi
12	Kick a dolryo cha-gi with the left leg (Kihop) and set the foot in the direction F.		
	Quickly turn around to the right and move the right foot in the direction of L3.	Orun ahp-gubi	Ahre maggi
13	Kick with the left leg—ahp cha-gi—and return the foot to the original position; the left foot is pulled back slightly for the dwi-gubi.	Owen dwi-gubi	Momtong bakkat maggi
14	Turn 180 degrees to the left on the right foot in the direction of R3.	Owen ahp-gubi	Ahre maggi
15	Kick with the right leg—ahp cha-gi—and place the foot back in the original position; the left foot is pulled back slightly for the dwi-gubi.	Orun dwi-gubi	Momtong bakkat maggi
16	Turn on the left foot in the direction F, but move the right back in the direction B.	Orun dwi-gubi	Son-nal momtong maggi
17	Continue looking in the direction F while moving the left foot back in the direction B.	Owen dwi-gubi	Son-nal momtong maggi
18	Move the right foot back one step in the direction B.	Owen ahp-gubi	Batangson momtong maggi (then quickly) momtong baro ji-ru-gi
	Position of the feet remains unchanged.		
19	Continue looking in the direction F, but move the left foot in the direction B.	Orun ahp-gubi	Batangson momtong maggi (then quickly) momtong baro ji-ru-gi
	Position of the feet remains unchanged.		
Guman	Pull the right foot back to the left foot, and look in the direction F.	Naranhi sogi	Gibon junbi

Tae-Kook 7 Chang

	Body and Leg Movements	Stance	Hand Techniques
Junbi	Look in the direction F, and step sideways with the left foot.	Naranhi sogi	Gibon junbi
1	Turn to your left in the direction of L1.	Owen poom sogi	Batangson momtong an maggi
2	Kick with the right leg—ahp cha-gi—returning the foot to its starting place.	Owen poom sogi	Momtong maggi
3	Turn 180 degrees to the right on your left leg in the direction of R1.	Orun poom sogi	Batangson momtong an maggi
4	Kick with the left leg—ahp cha-gi—returning the foot to its starting place.	Orun poom sogi	Momtong maggi
5	Move the left foot forward in the direction F without changing the position of the right foot.	Orun dwi-gubi	Son-nal ahre maggi
6	Move the right foot forward in the direction F.	Owen dwi-gubi	Son-nal ahre maggi
7	Move the left foot forward in the direction of L2 without changing the position of the right foot.	Owen poom sogi	Guduro batangson momtong an maggi
8	Stance remains unchanged.	Owen poom sogi	Orun dung-joomok ahp chi-gi (quickly)
9	Turn in place to your right in the direction of R2.	Orun poom sogi	Guduro batangson momtong an maggi
10	Stance remains unchanged.	Orun poom sogi	Owen dung-joomok ahp chi-gi
11	Straighten your body while pulling the left foot towards the right without moving the right foot—modum-baal—and look in the direction F.	Moa sogi	Bo-joomok (in front of the neck)
12	Move the left foot forward in the direction F.	Owen ahp-gubi	Dubon gawi maggi 1. Bandae gawi maggi (such as) orun bakkat palmok ahre maggi (and) owen an palmok bakkat momtong maggi; 2. Gawi maggi (quickly twice in a row)
13	Move the right foot forward one step in the direction F.	Orun ahp-gubi	Dubon gawi maggi (in rapid succession)

Continued on following pages.

Tae-Kook 7 Chang

	Body and Leg Movements	Stance	Hand Techniques
14	Turn left on the ball of the right foot, moving the left foot in the direction of R3.	Owen ahp-gubi	Momtong hecho maggi
15	Forcefully pull the right knee up for a **moorup chi-gi**, and jump quickly one step forward in the direction of R3.	Orun koa sogi	Momtong hecho ji-ru-gi
16	Keep the right foot in place, and move only the left foot back while continuing to look in the direction of R3.	Orun ahp-gubi	Otgoro ahre maggi
17	Turn 180 degrees to the right on the ball of the left foot, moving the left foot in the direction of L3.	Orun ahp-gubi	Momtong hecho maggi
18	Forcefully pull the left knee up for a **moorup chi-gi**, jumping quickly one step forward in the direction of L3.	Owen koa sogi	Momtong jechyo ji-ru-gi (quickly)
19	Keep the left foot in place, and move the right foot back while continuing to look in the direction of L3.	Owen ahp-gubi	Otgoro ahre maggi
20	Straighten your body, and move the left foot forward in the direction B.	Owen ahp sogi	Owen dung-joomok eolgul bakkat chi-gi
21	Kick with the right leg against an outstretched left hand—pyojok cha-gi—while continuing to look in the direction B.	Juchoom sogi	Orun palkoop pyojok chi-gi (→ B)
22	Keep the right foot in place and straighten your body, then pull your right foot in.	Orun ahp sogi	Orun dung-joomok eolgul bakkat chi-gi
23	Kick with the left leg against an outstretched right hand—pyojok chi-gi—placing the foot on the ground in the direction B.	Juchoom sogi	Owen palkoop pyojok ji-ru-gi (→ B)
24	Stance remains unchanged.	Juchoom sogi	Owen han son-nal momtong yop maggi
25	Move the right foot forward in the direction B.	Juchoom sogi	Orun yop chi-gi (Kihop)
Guman	Turn left on the ball of the right foot, and look in the direction F.	Naranhi sogi	Gibon junbi

Tae-Kook 8 Chang

	Body and Leg Movements	Stance	Hand Techniques
Junbi	Look in the direction F, and pull the left foot towards the right.	Naranhi sogi	Gibon junbi
1	Move the left foot forward in the direction F.	Orun dwi-gubi	Guduro momtong bakkat maggi
2	Move the right foot forward in the direction F.	Owen ahp-gubi	Momtong baro ji-ru-gi
3	With the left leg kick a **du-baaldung song ahp cha-gi** by jumping forward in the direction F (Kihop).	Owen ahp-gubi	Momtong maggi (then) momtong dubon ji-ru-gi
4	Move the right foot forward in the direction F.	Orun ahp-gubi	Momtong bandae ji-ru-gi
5	Turn left on the ball of the right foot until you are able to place the left foot in the direction of **R3**; your head is turned in the direction of **R3**.	Orun ahp-gubi	Owen-santul maggi
6	Change your position by turning in the direction of **R3**.	(Change) Owen ahp-gubi	Orun joomok dangyo tok ji-ru-gi (slow)
7	Pull the left foot in the direction of **L3** in front of the right foot, changing your center of gravity for **owen ahp koa sogi**; then move the right foot one step in the direction of **L3**; head is turned in the direction of **L3**.	Owen ahp-gubi (looking → L3)	Owen-santul maggi
8	Turn your body to the right without moving your feet, while continuing to look in the direction of **L3**.	(Change) Orun ahp-gubi	Owen joomok dangyo tok ji-ru-gi (slow)
9	Turn to the left on the ball of the left foot, placing the right foot in the direction B; look in the direction F.	Orun dwi-gubi	Son-nal momtong maggi
10	Move the left foot slightly forward without changing the position of the right foot.	Owen ahp-gubi	Momtong baro ji-ru-gi

116

Continued on following pages.

	Body and Leg Movements	Stance	Hand Techniques
11	Kick with the right leg—ahp cha-gi—returning the foot to its starting place; then quickly move the left foot one step back, pulling the left foot closer to the right.	Orun poom sogi	Batangson momtong maggi
12	Move the left foot forward in the direction of L2.	Owen poom sogi	Son-nal momtong maggi
13	The right foot remains in place while you kick with the left leg—ahp cha-gi—setting the foot on the ground in the direction of L3.	Owen ahp-gubi	Momtong baro ji-ru-gi
14	Pull the left foot closer to the right without moving the right foot.	Owen poom sogi	Batangson momtong maggi
15	Turn the body 180 degrees to the right on the left foot in the direction of R2.	Orun poom sogi	Son-nal momtong maggi
16	The left foot remains in place while you kick with the right leg—ahp cha-gi—setting the foot on the ground in the direction of R2.	Orun ahp-gubi	Momtong baro ji-ru-gi
17	Pull the right foot closer to the left without moving the left foot.	Orun poom sogi	Batangson momtong maggi
18	Turn to your left, and place the right foot in the direction B without moving the left foot.	Owen dwi-gubi	Guduro ahre maggi ($\rightarrow$ B)
19	Kick with the left leg—ahp cha-gi—without moving the right foot; then quickly carry out a jumping kick—ahp cha-gi—with the right foot while remaining in place (the left foot must land where the right foot had been) (Kihop).	Orun ahp-gubi	Momtong maggi (then) owen-orun momtong ji-ru-gi

Continued on following pages.

	Body and Leg Movements	Stance	Hand Techniques
20	Turn to the left on the ball of the right foot, placing the left foot in the direction of L1.	Orun dwi-gubi	Han son-nal momtong yop maggi
21	Move the left foot forward in the direction of L1.	(Change) owen ahp-gubi	Orun palkoop eolgul dolryo ji-ru-gi
22	Stance remains unchanged.	Owen ahp-gubi	Orun dung-joomok ahp chi-gi
23	Stance remains unchanged.	Orun ahp-gubi	Momtong bandae ji-ru-gi
24	Turn 180 degrees to the right on the left leg in the direction of R1, moving the right foot slightly to the left.	Owen dwi-gubi	Han son-nal mómtong yop maggi
25	Push the right foot slightly forward in the direction of R1.	Orun ahp-gubi	Owen palkoop eolgul dolryo chi-gi
26	Stance remains unchanged.	Orun ahp-gubi	Owen dung-joomok eolgul ahp chi-gi
27	Stance remains unchanged.	Orun ahp-gubi	Momtong bandae ji-ru-gi
Guman	Pull the left foot towards the right, and turn left in the direction F.	Naranhi sogi	Gibon junbi

Koryo

	Body and Leg Movements	Stance	Hand Techniques
Junbi	Look in the direction F, and move the left foot to the side; lift your hand to your chin.	Naranhi sogi	Tongmilgi junbi
1	Turn to your left, and move the left foot in the direction of L1.	Orun dwi-gubi	Son-nal momtong maggi
2	While keeping the left foot in place, kick with the right foot at knee-height—ahre yop cha-gi—and then a momtong yop cha-gi in the direction of L1; place the foot on the ground in the same direction.	Orun ahp-gubi	Son-nal bakkat chi-gi
3	Stance and body position remain the same.	Orun ahp-gubi	Momtong baro ji-ru-gi
4	Pull the right foot back a little; the left foot does not move.	Owen ahp-gubi	Momtong maggi
5	Turn 180 degrees to the right on the ball of the left foot, moving the right foot one step forward in the direction of R1.	Owen dwi-gubi	Son-nal momtong maggi
6	While the right foot remains in place, kick with the left leg—ahre yop cha-gi—and then a momtong yop cha-gi in the direction of R1; set the foot on the ground pointing in the same direction.	Owen ahp-gubi	Son-nal bakkat chi-gi
7	Stance remains unchanged.	Owen ahp-gubi	Momtong baro ji-ru-gi
8	Pull the left foot back a little while the right remains in place.	Orun ahp-gubi	Momtong maggi
9	Turn to the left on the ball of the right foot, moving the left foot forward in the direction F—carrying out an owen han son-nal ahre maggi.	Owen ahp-gubi	Orun kal-jabi

Continued on following pages.

Koryo

	Body and Leg Movements	Stance	Hand Techniques
10	Kick with the right leg—ahp cha-gi—placing the right foot down in the direction F, while carrying out an **orun han son-nal ahre maggi.**	Orun ahp-gubi	Owen kal-jabi
11	Kick with the left leg—ahp cha-gi—setting the left foot down in the direction F, while carrying out an **owen han son-nal ahre maggi.**	Owen ahp-gubi	Orun kal-jabi (Kihop)
12	Kick with the right leg—ahp cha-gi—setting the foot down in the direction F.	Orun ahp-gubi	Moorup kokki
13	Turn 180 degrees on the right foot until you can place the right foot down in the direction F; look in the direction B; the right foot is in front.	Orun ahp-gubi	An palmok momtong hecho maggi
14	Kick with the left leg—ahp cha-gi—setting the foot down in the direction B.	Owen ahp-gubi	Moorup kokki
15	Move the left foot back a little, while the right foot remains in place.	Owen ahp sogi	An palmok momtong hecho maggi
16	Turn right on the ball of the left foot until the right foot points in the direction of R2; look in the direction of L2.	Juchoom sogi	Owen han son-nal yop maggi
17	Stance remains unchanged.	Juchoom sogi	Orun joomok pyomok ji-ru-gi
18	Cross the right foot over the left—koa sogi—while at the same time the hands are placed on the side of the waist that faces R2; weight is balanced on the right foot while you kick the left leg—yop cha-gi—in the direction of R2; at the conclusion you are looking in the direction of R2.	Orun ahp-gubi	Owen pyong sonkut ahre jechyo ji-ru-gi
19	Move the right foot back a little while the left foot remains in place.	Orun ahp sogi	Ahre maggi
20	Move the left foot forward one step in the direction of R2 while carrying out an **owen batangson momtong nullo maggi;** then quickly move the right foot one step forward.	Juchoom sogi	Orun palkoop yop chi-gi (→ R2)

124

Continued on following pages.

	Body and Leg Movements	Stance	Hand Techniques
21	Stance remains unchanged.	Juchoom sogi	Orun han son-nal momtong yop maggi
22	Stance remains unchanged.	Juchoom sogi	Owen joomok pyojok ji-ru-gi
23	Cross the left foot in front over the right foot for an **ahp koa sogi**; shift your body weight to the left foot and kick with the right leg—**ahp cha-gi**—in the direction of R2; the right foot is then set on the ground in this direction while you also turn the body in the direction of L2.	Owen ahp-gubi	Orun pyong-sonkut ahre jechyo chi-ru-gi
24	Move the left foot back a little while the right foot remains in place.	Owen ahp sogi	Ahre maggi
25	Move the right foot forward in the direction of L2 while carrying out an **orun batangson momtong nullo maggi**—quickly moving the left foot forward one step.	Juchoom sogi	Owen palkoop yop chi-gi
26	Lift both hands over your head and in a circular motion move them to the outside and down again; move the left foot towards the right for a **modum-baal**.	Moa sogi	Owen me-joomok ahre pyojok chi-gi ($\rightarrow$ F)
27	Turn left on the right foot, and move the right foot one step forward in the direction B while carrying out an **owen han son-nal bakkat chi-gi**.	Owen ahp-gubi	Owen han son-nal ahre maggi
28	Move the right foot forward in the direction B while carrying out an **orun han son-nal mok chi-gi**.	Orun ahp-gubi	Owen han son-nal ahre maggi
29	Move the left foot forward one step in the direction B while carrying out an **owen han son-nal mok chi-gi**.	Owen ahp-gubi	Owen han son-nal ahre maggi
30	Move the left foot forward one step in the direction B.	Orun ahp-gubi	Orun kal-jabi (Kihop)
Guman	Turn left on the ball of the right foot until you are able to look in the direction F.	Naranhi sogi	Tongmilgi jumbi

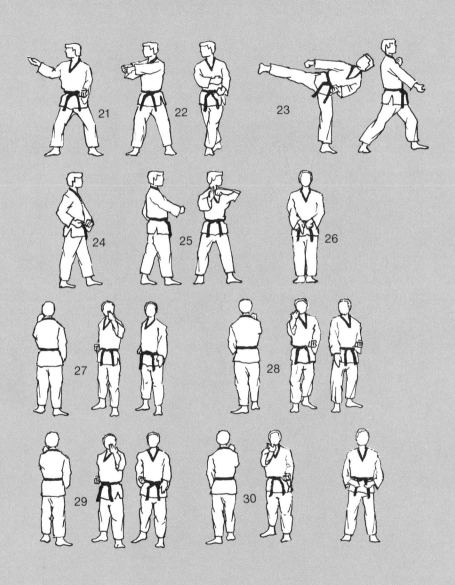

Kum-Kang

	Body and Leg Movements	Stance	Hand Techniques
Junbi	Look in the direction F, and move the left foot sideways.	Naranhi sogi	Gibon junbi
1	Move the left foot forward in the direction F.	Owen ahp-gubi	An palmok momtong hecho maggi
2	Move the right foot forward one step.	Orun ahp-gubi	Orun batangson tok chi-gi
3	Move the left foot forward one step.	Owen ahp-gubi	Owen batangson tok chi-gi
4	Move the right foot forward one step.	Orun ahp-gubi	Orun batangson tok chi-gi
5	Move the right foot back a little without moving the left foot; continue to look in the direction F.	Orun dwi-gubi	Han son-nal momtong maggi
6	Move the left foot back one step in the direction B.	Owen dwi-gubi	Han son-nal momtong maggi
7	Move the right foot back one step in the direction B.	Orun dwi-gubi	Han son-nal momtong maggi
8	While the right foot remains in place, pull the left leg up for a **hakdari sogi**; at the same time move the left arm up slowly and the right arm down—also slowly but with power; look in the direction L.	Orun hakdari sogi	Kum-kang maggi
9	Move the left foot in the direction L and one step to the side.	Juchoom sogi	Owen kun dolchogwi ($\rightarrow$ R)

128

Continued on following pages.

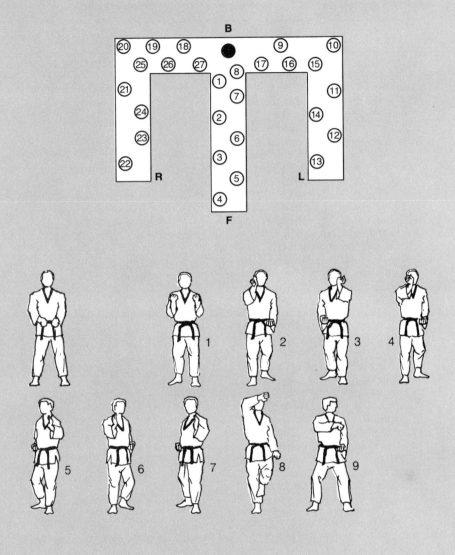

Kum-Kang

	Body and Leg Movements	Stance	Hand Techniques
10	Turn left on the left foot; move the right foot in the direction L, and then turn around 360 degrees until the left foot can again be set firmly on the ground in the direction L.	Juchoom sogi	Owen kun dolchogwi ($\rightarrow$ L)
11	Turn left on the ball of the left foot, and plant the left foot with force on the ground in the direction F.	Juchoom sogi	Santul maggi (look $\rightarrow$ F) (Kihop)
12	Turn right on the ball of the right foot until you can place the foot in the direction F.	Juchoom sogi	An palmok momtong hecho maggi (quickly)
13	While the right foot remains in place, pull the left foot closer to the right; hands are crossed in front of the chest and arms are moved down slowly but forcefully in a circular movement; exhale slowly throughout this movement.	Naranhi sogi	Ahre hecho maggi (look $\rightarrow$ R)
14	Turn right on the ball of the right foot, and set the left foot forcefully in the direction B.	Juchoom sogi	Santul maggi
15	Turn 180 degrees to the right on the ball of the left foot, pulling the left foot up for a hakdari sogi.	Owen hakdari sogi	Kum-kang maggi (slowly but carried out with force; look $\rightarrow$ R)
16	While the left foot remains in place, move the right foot quickly one step in the direction R.	Juchoom sogi	Orun kun dolchogwi (look $\rightarrow$ R)
17	Turn to the right on the right foot; move the left foot in the direction R and make a 360-degree turn until the right foot can again be set on the ground in the direction R; carry out the movement quickly.	Juchoom sogi	Orun kun dolchogwi

130

Continued on following pages.

	Body and Leg Movements	Stance	Hand Techniques
18	Pull the right foot up to do a **hakdari sogi**.	Orun hakdari sogi	Kum-kang maggi (slowly but with force)
19	Move the right foot forward in the direction **R**.	Juchoom sogi	Orun kun dolchogwi
20	Turn to the right on the ball of the right foot; point the left foot in the direction of **R** and then make a 360-degree turn, placing the left foot back in the previous position (**R**).	Juchoom sogi	Orun kun dolchogwi
21	Turn to the right on the ball of the right foot until you are able to set the left foot on the ground in the direction **F**.	Juchoom sogi	Santul maggi (Kihop) (look → R)
22	Turn to the left on the ball of the left foot, placing the right foot in the direction **F**.	Juchoom sogi	An palmok momtong hecho maggi (move quickly, look → L)
23	Move the left foot a little to the right; the right foot stays in place.	Naranhi sogi	Ahre hecho maggi
24	Turn left on the ball of the left foot, and forcefully place the right foot on the ground pointing in the direction **B**.	Juchoom sogi	Santul maggi
25	Turn to the left on the ball of the right foot, and pull the left foot up for a **hakdari sogi**.	Orun hakdari sogi	Kum-kang maggi (slower but with force; look → L)
26	Quickly move the left foot one step forward in the direction L; the right foot remains in place.	Juchoom sogi	Owen kun dolchogwi (look → L)
27	Turn left on the ball of the left foot; point the right foot in the direction L and turn around 360 degrees until the left foot can be placed on the ground at its starting place.	Juchoom sogi	Owen kun dolchogwi (look → F)
Guman	Pull the left foot slightly towards the right foot.	Naranhi sogi	Gibon junbi

	Body and Leg Movements	Stance	Hand Techniques
Junbi	Look in the direction F, and move the left foot sideways.	Naranhi sogi	Gibon junbi
1	Turn to the left and move the right foot forward in the direction of **L1**.	Owen poom sogi	Son-nal ahre hecho maggi (right to left)
2	Kick with the right leg—ahp cha-gi—placing the foot one step forward in the direction of **R1**.	Orun poom sogi	Son-nal ahre hecho maggi
4	Kick with the left leg—ahp cha-gi—placing the foot on the ground in the direction of **R1**.	Owen ahp-gubi	Momtong dubon ji-ru-gi
5	Turn left on the ball of the right foot.	Owen ahp-gubi	Jebipum mok chi-gi
6	Pull the right hand (palm pointing down) towards the body; then move the right foot one step forward in the direction F.	Orun ahp-gubi	Momtong baro ji-ru-gi
7	Open the left hand (palm pointing down) towards the body; then move the right foot one step forward in the direction F.	Owen ahp-gubi	Momtong baro ji-ru-gi
8	Open the right hand (palm pointing down) towards the body; then move the right foot one step forward in the direction F.	Orun ahp-gubi	Momtong baro ji-ru-gi (Kihop)

134

Continued on following pages.

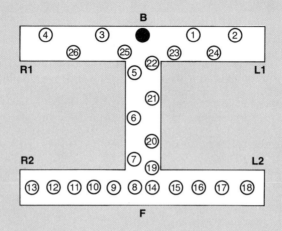

Tae-Book

	Body and Leg Movements	Stance	Hand Techniques
9	Turn to the left on the ball of the right foot, moving the left foot forward in the direction of R2.	Orun dwi-gubi	Kum-kang momtong maggi
10	Body position and stance remain unchanged.	Orun dwi-gubi	Dangyo tok ji-ru-gi
11	Body position and stance remain unchanged.	Orun dwi-gubi	Owen joomok yop ji-ru-gi
12	Body position and stance remain unchanged.	Orun hakdari sogi	Orun jagun dolchogwi
13	Kick with the left leg—yop cha-gi—moving the left foot one step forward in the direction of R2.	Owen ahp-gubi	Orun palkoop pyojok chi-gi
14	Turn around to the right in the direction of L2, pulling the left foot towards the right for a **moa sogi**. Immediately move the right foot one step forward in the direction of L2.	Owen dwi-gubi	Kum-kang momtong maggi
15	Body position and stance remain unchanged	Owen dwi-gubi	Dangyo tok ji-ru-gi
16	Body position and stance remain unchanged.	Owen dwi-gubi	Orun joomok yop ji-ru-gi
17	Lift the right foot to the left knee.	Owen hakdari sogi	Owen jagun dolchogwi

136

Continued on following pages.

	Body and Leg Movements	Stance	Hand Techniques
18	Kick with the right leg—yop cha-gi—moving the foot one step forward in the direction of L2.	Orun ahp-gubi	Owen palkoop pyojok chi-gi
19	Pull the right foot towards the left for a **moa sogi**; immediately move the left foot one step forward in the direction B.	Orun dwi-gubi	Son-nal momtong maggi
20	Move the right foot forward one step in the direction B.	Orun ahp-gubi	Pyong sonkut sewo chi-ru-gi
21	Turn left on the ball of the right foot, then pull the left foot in front of and past the right foot until—after a 360-degree turn—the foot can be placed on the ground in the direction B.	Orun dwi-gubi	Owen dung-joomok eolgul bakkat chi-gi
22	Move the right foot forward one step in the direction B.	Orun ahp-gubi	Momtong bandae ji-ru-gi (Kihop)
23	Turn left on the ball of the right foot, moving the foot forward along the ground in the direction of L1; when carrying out the **gawi maggi**, the left hand is performing an **ahre maggi**.	Owen ahp-gubi	Gawi maggi
24	Kick with the right leg—ahp cha-gi—and then place the foot one step forward in the direction of L1.	Orun ahp-gubi	Momtong dubon ji-ru-gi
25	Turn 180 degrees to the right on the ball of the left foot, placing the right foot on the ground in the direction of R1; when carrying out the **gawi maggi**, the right hand is performing an **ahre maggi**.	Orun ahp-gubi	Gawi maggi
26	Kick with the left leg—ahp cha-gi—setting the foot down in the direction of R1.	Owen ahp-gubi	Momtong dubon ji-ru-gi
Guman	Turn to the left on the ball of the right foot until the left foot can be set down in the direction of L1—next to the right foot; look in the direction F.	Naranhi sogi	Gibon junbi

Glossary of Korean Terms

Ahp Front
Ahp cha-gi Front kick
Ahp-gubi sogi Forward stance
Ahp-koa sogi Cross stance, to the side
Ahp sogi Walking stance
Ahre Lower body (below the navel)
Ahre maggi Low block
An chi-gi Strike to the inside
An maggi Inside block

Baal Foot
Baal-badak Sole of foot
Baal-dung Instep
Baal-jit Step
Baal-nal Outside edge of foot
Bakkat From inside out
Bam-joomok Fist with knuckles pointed forward
Bandae ji-ru-gi Reverse punch
Baro Even, straight or "Return to initial position" command
Baro ji-ru-gi Walking punch
Batangson Ball of the thumb
Bato cha-gi Counterkick
Bikyo baal-jit Diagonal step
Bituro maggi Reverse block
Bo-joomok Left hand grabbing right fist

Cha-gi Kick, hit with foot
Cha-olligi Outstretched leg swung sideways
Cha-ryot "Stand at attention" command
Cha-ryot sogi Attention stance (V stance)
Chi-gi Strike, hit with hand
Chi ji-ru-gi Uppercut punch
Chi-ru-gi Fingertip thrust
Chung sung "Blue is the winner"

Dan 1st to 9th degree, master (15 years old and older)
Dangyo ji-ru-gi Pulling hit
Danjon Diaphragm
Dari Leg
Deuk-jeom A scored point

Dobok Tae kwon do uniform
Dolchogwi Hinge
Dolryo cha-gi Round kick
Dong-jak One single movement
Dubon Twice in a row
Dullo baal-jit Step by lifting foot
Dung-joomok chi-gi Back-of-fist punch
Dwi Back, backwards
Dwi cha-gi Back kick
Dwi-dolla baal-jit Backward turning step
Dwi-dolryo cha-gi Backward turning kick
Dwi-gubi sogi Back stance

Eolgul Face

Gam-jeom Deduction penalty
Gawi maggi Scissor block
Gibon Ground
Godub cha-gi Double hit with foot
Guduro-ahre maggi Low block with support
Guduro-eolgul maggi Face block with support
Guduro-momtong maggi Body block with support
Guligi cha-gi Hook kick
Guman sogi Closing stance, end of exercise
Gup Class, student level (10 to 1 Gup)
Gyop-son Hands placed on top of each other
Gyroogi Sparring

Hakdari sogi Crane stance
Hecho maggi Spreading block
Hong sung "Red is the winner"
Hosinsool The art of self-defense
Huryo cha-gi Wheel kick

Jagun Small
Jayu gyroogi Freestyle sparring
Jebipum Bird form
Jechyo ji-ru-gi Punch with turned fist

Jeon A round of competition
Ji-ru-gi Punch with fist
Joomok Fist, with pointing knuckles of index and middle fingers
Joo sim Referee
Juchoom sogi Horseback stance
Junbi "Prepare" command
Junbi sogi Preparation stance

Kal-jabi Knife hit
Kalyeo "Break" (stop during a match) command
Koa baal-jit Cross step
Koa sogi Twisted stance
Konggyokki Attacking techniques
Kullo baal-jit Foot-pulling step
Kullomoa baal-jit Switch step
Kum-kang maggi Combination face block and low side block, both hands
Kun Large
Kyesok "Continue fight" command
Kyonggo Warning
Kyorumse Basic fighting stance
Kyukpa Breaking technique or test

Maggi Blocking defensive motion
Me-joomok chi-gi Hammer-fist strike
Mikurum-baal Feet sliding
Mituro Downward
Moa baal-jit Closing step
Moa sogi Closed stance
Modum-baal; Legs closed
Mojuchoom sogi Horseback stance with legs turned 45 degrees
Mo-li Head
Mom Body
Momtong Trunk, collarbone to navel, of body
Momtong ji-ru-gi Middle punch
Momtong maggi Body block
Momtong yop maggi Side body block
Monge Locked hold
Moorup Knee

141

Glossary

Moorup kokki Striking opponent's knee with edge of hand or foot
Mullo baal-jit Back step
Myong-chi Solar plexus

Naeryo Downward
Naga baal-jit Starting step
Naranhi sogi Open parallel stance
Natchumse Low stance
Nullo maggi Downward block with ball of hand

Orun Right
Otgoro-ahre maggi Low cross block
Otgoro-eolgul maggi Face cross block
Owen Left
Owen-santul maggi Combination low block and inside-out face block, both hands

Paegi Release
Pal Arm
Palkoop chi-gi Elbow punch
Palmok Forearm
Poom Movement form, also the red/black degree for under age 15
Poomse Combination of movement forms against imaginary opponent
Poom sogi Tiger stance
Pyojok Target, direction
Pyong-hi sogi Ready stance
Pyon-joomok chi-gi Knuckle-fist punch

Sabomnim Master, instructor (above 4th dan)
Santul Mountain shape
Sewo chi-ru-gi Vertical thrust
Sewo-ji-ru-gi Vertical punch
Sogi Stance

Son Hand
Sonkut Fingertip
Sonmok Wrist
Son-nal chi-gi Knife-hand strike
Son-nal dung chi-gi Spear-fingers punch
Son-nal maggi Knife-hand block
Swio Standing relaxed, quiet

Tok Chin
Tongmilgi Squeeze an imaginary object in palm
Twi-o cha-gi Jumping kick
Ty Belt

Wee maggi Rising block
Wiro Upward

Yeot pero maggi Crossed (X) block
Yop cha-gi Side kick
Yop ji-ru-gi Side punch
Yop maggi Side block

Counting

one	hana	first	il
two	dul	second	le
three	set	third	sam
four	net	fourth	sa
five	dasot	fifth	oh
six	yasot	sixth	yuk
seven	elgub	seventh	chil
eight	yodol	eighth	pal
nine	ahob	ninth	gu
ten	yol	tenth	sib

Index

Advanced degree forms (*see Dan*)
Attitude, 16–17
Attacking Techniques (*Kong-gyokki*) (*see also specific kick or punch*)
  Feet/leg, 26–31
  Hand/arm, 26–28
  Overview, chart, 30–31

Back kick (*Dwi cha-gi*), 29
Backward turning kick (*Dwi-dolryo cha-gi*), 29
Balance, stability, 12
Belts (*Ty*), colors, chart, 5
Blocking (*see Maggi*)
Body, divisions
  Face (*Eolgul*), 15
  Lower body (*Ahre*), 15
  Trunk (*Momtong*), 15
Body punch (*Ji-ru-gi*), 27
Body strengthening, 17
Breaking technique (*Kyukpa*), 4, 15, 40
Breathing, 13–14, (*Yat*), 18

Character perfection (*Dok*), 16
Cheerfulness/happiness, Second (*Le*) chang, 48
Competition, 10
  Breaking technique (*Kyukpa*), 4, 15, 40
  Compulsory sparring (*Han-ben gyoroogi*), 5, 18, 32–33
  Freestyle sparring (*Jayu gy-oroogi*), 5, 15–16, 18
  Positions, 41–43
  Requirements for participants, 41
  Suggestions, 42–43
Concentration, 14
Coordination
  Mind/body, 5
  Nervous system, 13
Countertechniques, sequence of action, chart, 37–38

Dan, master level, exercises, 5, 15, 122–138

Defense
  Additional techniques, chart, 26
  Against being grabbed, 39
  Against choking attack, 39
  Against gripping, 39
  Against knife or club, 40
  Ancient form (*Taekyon*), 8
  Art of self-defense (*Hosinsool*), 4, 38–40
  Blocking (*Maggi*), 23–26
  Criteria of *Hosinsool*, 39
  Hwarang do (ancient art of fighting), 8–9
  Karate, 9
  Kung fu, 9
  Okinawate (early self-defense), 9
  Soo bak do (early martial art), 9–10
  Tactical response, 43
  Techniques, 25–26
Do, 4, 16–17
Dobok, 5
Dynamics, physics, 11–13

Eighth (*Pal*) chang (Earth), 49
Exercise forms, (*see Dan, Gup, and Poomse*)
Extremities as weapons, 7

Fifth (*Oh*) chang, 48
Fighting (*see* Competition)
Fighting stance, basic (*Kyo-rumse*), 41
Fire, third (*Sam*) chang, 48
First (*Il*) chang, 48
Formal exercises (*see Poomse*)
Fourth (*Sa*) chang, 48
Front kick (*Ahp cha-gi*), 28

Goals, 4, 6
Gup, student level, exercises, 5, 15, 45–46, 48–49, 50–120

Heavens/light, First (*Il*) chang, 48
Historical background, 8–10
Hwarang do (ancient art of fighting), 8–9

Karate, 9
Ki, 13
Kihop, 13–14
Knife-hand strike (*Son-nal chi-gi*), 28
Koryo (*see also Poomse*), 122–127
Kum-kang (*see also Poomse*), 128–133
Kung fu, 9

Maggi (Block), 23–26
  Body (*Momtong*), 24
  Face (*Eolgul*), 25
  Inside body (*Momtong an*), 25
  Knife-hand (*Son-nal*), 25–26
  Low (*Ahre*), 24
  Outside body (*Momtong bak-kat*), 25
  Spreading (*Hecho*), 26
Master level forms (*see Dan and Poomse*)
Master/instructor (*Sabom*), 18
Movements, sequence, 48–139
Movements system (*see Poomse*)

Newtonian principles
  Action equals reaction, 11
  Inertia, law of, 11
  Mechanics, law of, 11

Okinawate (early self-defense), 9

Pal-gwe (*see also Poomse*)
  1 *chang*, 50–53
  2 *chang*, 54–57
  3 *chang*, 58–61
  4 *chang*, 62–65
  5 *chang*, 66–71
  6 *chang*, 72–75
  7 *chang*, 76–79
  8 *chang*, 80–87
Paying respect (*Kyong-ye*), 18
Poomse (Exercise forms) (*see also Dan and Gup*)
  Chonkwon, 5, 15
  Criteria, 45
  Hansoo, 5, 15

Index

Ilyo, 5, 15
Jitae, 5, 15
Kihop, 18
Koryo, 5, 15, 45–46, 49, 122–126
Kum-Kang, 5, 15, 45, 47, 49, 128–132
Overview, chart, 45
Pal-gwe (1 to 8 *chang*), 5, 15, 45–46, 48–87
Performance, 45–139
Pyongwon, 5, 15
Sequences, chart, 31
Shipjin, 5, 15
Tae-book, 5, 15, 45, 47, 49, 134–139
Tae-kook (1 to 8 *chang*), 5, 15, 45–46, 48–49, 88–120
Power, concentrated (*Kihop*), 18

Reverse punch (*Bandae ji-ru-gi*), 27
Round kick (*Dolryo cha-gi*), 28

Second (*Le*) *chang*, 48
Self-confidence, 6
Self-defense art (*Hosinsool*) (*see* Defense)
Seventh (*Chil*) *chang*, 48
Side kick (*Yop cha-gi*), 28–29
Sixth (*Yuk*) *chang*, 48
Sogi (Stance), 19–23
  Attention (*Cha-ryot*), 20
  Back (*Dwi-gubi*), 22
  Basic fighting (*Kyorumse*), 20
  Closed (*Moa*), 20
  Crane (*Hakdari*), 22–23
  Forward (*Ahp-gubi*), 21
  Horseback (*Juchoom*), 21
  Open parallel (*Naranhi*), 21
  Ready (*Pyong-hi*), 20
  Tiger (*Poom*), 22

Twisted (*Koa*), 23
Walking (*Ahp*), 21
Soo bak do (early martial art), 9–10
Sparring (*Gyoroogi*)
  Basic principles, 33
  Compulsory (*Han-bon*), 5, 18, 32–33
  Freestyle (*Jayu*), 5, 15–16, 18
  Hand techniques, 33
  Movements, 33
  Practice protocol, 34
Speed, 12–13
Stamina, 17
Stance (*see Sogi*)
Stepping techniques (*Baal-jit-ki*), 35–37
Strength, mental, 47
Student forms (*see Gup and Poomse*)
Summit, mountain, seventh (*Chil*) *chang*, 48

Tactical response, 49
Tae-book (*see also Poomse*), 134–139
Tae-kook (*see also Poomse*)
  1 *chang*, 88–91
  2 *chang*, 92–95
  3 *chang*, 96–99
  4 *chang*, 100–103
  5 *chang*, 104–107
  6 *chang*, 108–111
  7 *chang*, 112–115
  8 *chang*, 116–121
Taekyon, ancient form, 8
Techniques
  Attacking (*Kyonggyokki*), 26–27, 30–31
  Basic skills, 19–31
  Blocking (*Maggi*), 23–26
  Combinations, 32–40

Countertechniques, 37–38
Feet/leg (*Cha-gi*), 27–31, 34–35
Gyoroogi (freestyle and compulsory sparring), 5, 15–16, 18, 32–33
Hand/arm, 26–28, 33–34
Kyukpa (Breaking technique), 4, 15, 40
Overview chart, 19
Poomse (Formal exercises), 5, 14–15, 18, 45–139
Punch with fist (*Ji-ru-gi*), 26–28
Stance (*Sogi*), 19–23
Stepping (*Baal-jit-ki*), 35–37
Steps (light and solid), 12–13
Strike with hand (*Chi-gi*), 27
Thrust with fingertips (*Chi-ru-gi*), 26
Training, and, 11–19
Third (*Sam*) *chang*, 48
Thunder, fourth (*Sa*) *chang*, 48
Tips, 4, 16, 41, 42, 43
Training
  athletics, 7
  basic, 14
  Conduct, 49
  Character development, 6
  Recommendations, 49
  Space (*Dojang*), 17–18
  Step-, 36
  Techniques and, 11–19
Turning, 14
Ty (Belts), colors, chart, 5

Uniform (*Dobok* or *Gi*), 5

Walking punch (*Baro ji-ru-gi*), 27
Water, sixth (*Yuk*) *chang*, 48
Weaponless defense, 4
Willpower, 6, 17
Wind, Fifth (*Oh*) *chang*, 48